D0930748

Res
E184
B67
C99

ETHNIC CHRONOLOGY SERIES
NUMBER 28

The Czechs in America
1633-1977
A Chronology & Fact Book

Compiled and edited by

Vera Laska

1978
OCEANA PUBLICATIONS, INC.
DOBBS FERRY, NEW YORK

APR 1 8 1978

201810

Library of Congress Cataloging in Publication Data
Main entry under title:

The Czechs in America, 1633-1977.

(Ethnic chronology series)
Bibliography: p.
Includes index.
SUMMARY: A history of the Czechs in the United
States in chronological format with a selection of
illustrative documents, appendices, and a bibliography.
    1.Czech Americans — History — Chronology. 2. Czech
Americans — History — Sources. [1. Czech Americans —
History] I. Laska, Vera,   II. Series.
E184.B67C99   973'.04'9186   77-20124
ISBN 0-379-00528-X

© Copyright 1978 by Oceana Publications, Inc.

All rights reserved. No part of this publication may be reproduced or transmitted in any form or by any means, electronic or mechanical, including photocopy, recording, xerography, or any information storage and re-trieval system, without permission in writing from the publisher.

Manufactured in the United States of America

To Iska and Jerry, Sonia and Joe.

TABLE OF CONTENTS

Their historical background helps explain the motivations and behavior of the Czechs who settled in America. Their Christian ruler Václav, known from the carol "Good King Wenceslas," died in 929 and became the first Czech saint. The Czechs and Moravians developed under western influence. "Bohemian" is synonymous with "Czech," the latter being the preferred modern usage. It denotes the inhabitants of both Bohemia and Moravia.

Jan Hus, rector of the university founded in 1348 in Prague, was a national as well as religious reformer. A century before Luther, he preached in his native tongue against the corruption in the church; he was burnt at the stake in 1415.

After the Battle on the White Mountain, in the year that the Pilgrims landed at Plymouth, the independence of the Czech Kingdom became restricted for three centuries. The counter-reformation forced hundreds of non-Catholics to leave the country, among them the bishop of the Unity of Brethren, Jan Amos Komenský (Comenius), father of modern education. They scattered in Poland, Hungary, Sweden, Holland and England. One group found refuge in Saxony. It was from this branch, by now Germanized, that in the early 18th century immigrants set out for America as Moravian Brethren.

A few individuals reached the New World in early colonial times, and the Moravians belong at least ideologically into the Czech group, although there were more Germans than Czechs among them. Czechs started arriving in larger numbers after the 1848 revolution. By the 1880's the group was well established. The awakening nationalism in the mother country was mirrored in the Czech communities in the United States. As the Catholic Church had been a tool of the oppressive Austrian state, the resentment against both manifested itself the moment the Czechs reached the free shores of America: at least half of them left the church. This helps explain the large number of freethinkers among them. A radical faction were atheists, but the majority of freethinkers were agnostics, and their ideologies corresponded to those of Franklin and Jefferson as well as to those of Tom Paine.

The Czechs have been deeply loyal to their new homeland. Their press facilitated naturalization. Yet they were also ardent Czech patriots, as is clearly evident from their publications. In a free atmosphere they spoke out for their muzzled former compatriots and blasted in no uncertain terms the Hapsburg Kaiser.

It was with the moral and financial support of their kinsmen in America, that the Czechs during World War I

regained their independence, and after World War II
achieved freedom from nazism. In the former case, the
liberation movement was led by professor Tomáš Masaryk,
who had an American wife. The agreement of the Czechs
and Slovaks - who for the last thousand years were under
Hungarian rule - to join together in forming the Czechoslovak Republic, was formally signed in Pittsburgh, their
Declaration of Independence in Washington, D. C.

The motivations of the Czech immigrants up to World
War I were economic and partially political. During the
20th century three smaller waves of refugees came through
the "golden door," all three characterized by a large
proportion of intellectuals seeking freedom as a consequence of the political events of 1938, 1948 and 1968.
In the case of 1938 the expelling force was combined
with religious persecution of Czechs of the Jewish faith.

The Czech immigrants came with their families; they
came to stay. They were settlers, not seekers of dollars
to be repatriated. They were mostly simple farmers, laborers, artisans and tradesmen, hoping to own their own
homes. They contributed to the mainstream of America
not only as hewers of wood and drawers of water, but also their skills, music and humor. They brought as a
dowry their traditional respect and love for learning
and for freedom of conscience. It is significant that
the three national leaders, Hus, Komenský and Masaryk,
were teachers and protestants [small p intentional].
The nation produced a St. Wenceslas but also a Švejk,
the "New World Symphony" as well as the "Beer Barrel
Polka."

The characteristic features of Czech immigration to
America were:

A high percentage of skilled labor and literacy rate.

The ideological division between Catholics and freethinkers, much more pronounced in America than in the
homeland. This contributed to a duplication of fraternal
and cultural organizations, the benefit of which to the
Czechs or to America is highly debatable.

From America the group contributed immeasurably to
the creation of an independent republic in the former
homeland by lobbying to influence American public opinion
and by financing the liberation of the country, whose
Declaration of Independence and Constitution bear striking similarities to the American documents of freedom.

Vera Laska
Regis College
Weston, Massachusetts

1600's   The earliest history of Czech immigrants to
            America is fragmentary at best. Many hund-
            red Protestants fled from their homeland af-
            ter 1620 to Sweden, Holland, and England,
            and some of them came over to America with
            those national groups. A few ship and church
            records testify of the mere existence of in-
            dividuals in those early days in the colonies.

            Early Spanish mission bells in the southwest
            bear names of Czech saints; this purely cir-
            cumstantial evidence indicates that there
            might have been Czechs there before the Mexi-
            can territories became parts of the U. S.

1620's   The Dutch government sent out Mr. Loketka to
            report on the state of their colonies. He
            accomplished his mission, but it is not known
            whether he remained in America.

1633   Augustine Herrman (1605-1686) from Mšeno, son
            of a pastor of the Brethren, was the first
            Czech immigrant known by name to settle in
            America. He came in the employ of Peter
            Gabry and Sons of Amsterdam to New Amsterdam.
            He was a surveyor and one of the first found-
            ers of the Virginia tobacco trade. He owned
            a home in what later became Pearl Street.

1635   The ship Expedition sailing to Barbados had
            on board Edward Beneš.

1637   Blacksmith Joris from Silesia arrived in New
            Netherland.

1638   March 29. Czech Protestant exiles were among
            the 23 Swedish soldiers and two officers who
            arrived on the Kalmar Nyckel under Peter
            Minuit and built Fort Christina on the tri-
            butary of the Delaware River. Since fifty
            exiled Czech nobles were in the employ of
            the Swedish armies, it is more than likely
            that others arrived on subsequent expeditions
            to New Sweden, especially as its governor,
            Johan Printz, who came in 1643, was a mili-
            tary man.

1639   December 18. Citizen Joris of New Amsterdam
            married Swedish Engeltje Mans and settled at
            Dutch Kills, where later a large Czech set-
            tlement arose.

1642   According to Cotton Mather's _Magnalia Christi Americana_ (1702), Ján Amos Komenský (Comenius, 1592-1670), the exiled bishop of the Czech Brethren and the father of modern education, was invited to become president of Harvard College by John Winthrop, son of the Massachusetts governor. Komenský recommended universal education for both sexes and used visual aids; had he come, American education would have been revolutionized. He went to Sweden instead.

1645   February 26. Jeuriaen [Jiří?] Fradell of Moravia married Tryn Herxker; he received as her dowry land on Long Island, east of Hellgate (Hell Gate).

1647   May 11 (?). Frederick Philipse, Protestant exile from Bohemia, to whom chroniclers refer as the "Bohemian Merchant Prince," arrived in New Amsterdam; if he came on the same ship with Peter Stuyvesant, he sailed from Holland via Curacao. Some consider him a descendant of the Counts Kinský. In 1653 he appraised Augustine Herrman's property, which indicates that they knew each other. Philipse owned tobacco planations on Barbados and tracts of land in Westchester and Putnam Counties. He erected Philips Manor in Yonkers and Philips Castle at Sleepy Hollow, where he lies buried. He died in 1701.

          Philips Manor is the location of R. N. Stephens' novel _The Continental Dragon_. Young George Washington showed interest in a descendant of Frederick Philipse, Mary Philips, immortalized in James Fenimore Cooper's novel _The Spy_.

1650   John Duch settled in Northumberland County, Virginia.

1651   December 10. Augustine Herrman married Joan Varleth from Utrecht in New Amsterdam.

1652   Anne Dubeš owned land in Lancaster County, Pennsylvania [?].

1653   Anna Simko settled in Northumberland County, Virginia.

1654   Matthew Cenig [Čeněk] died in Boston.

1655 Christopher Donák and his family purchased
land in Northampton County, Virginia. John
Doza, his fellow passenger, settled nearby.

May 14. S. Herrmans was married in the Dutch
Church in New Amsterdam; this could have been
one of Augustine Herrman's three sisters.

John Kostlo resided in New Amsterdam.

Elisabeth Baysa, Mary Bunc and Louis Standla
lived in Hartford, Connecticut.

1656 Augustine Herrman executed the first sketch
of New Amsterdam, which had 1000 inhabitants.

1659 Herrman was sent by governor Stuyvesant to
settle the border dispute between the Dutch
of New York and the English in Maryland. He
had proven his negotiating talents before,
on a similar mission to Massachusetts regarding Indian hostilities.

1660 For preparing the first map of Maryland and
Virginia [original in British Museum, copy
at Library of Congress], Herrman obtained
from Lord Baltimore a 20,000 acre land grant
at the junction of the Elk and Bohemia rivers
near Chesapeake Bay, in Cecil and New Castle
Counties. He moved to Maryland and built
Bohemia Manor. He acquired additional land
grants, which he named after his daughters
The Three Bohemian Sisters and Little Bohemia. He intended to plant a colony to be
called New Bohemia. In his will he made
provision for a Protestant school in Maryland.

Herrmanville in Maryland was named after him.
It is said that the following families trace
their ancestry to Herrman's three daughters:
Bayard, Boudley, Chew, French, Gordon, Hore,
Howard, Jekyll, Jennings, Mifflin, Neal,
Randolph, Ridgely, Shannon, Shippen, Spencer,
Thompson, Trent, Van der Heyden and Yeates.

September 12. Adam Unkelba was married in
the Dutch Church in New Amsterdam.

1679 July 15. Albrecht [Albert?] Zaborowsky
signed as interpreter an Indian treaty in
New York. He is considered the ancestor of
the New England Zabriskie family. Was he
Záborovský, a Czech, or Zaborowski, a Pole?
The signature can be read both ways.

The Bohemian language had been recorded as
one of the dozen languages spoken in New
York in the second half of the 17th century.

December 22. The "True and Perfect List of
all ye Names of ye Inhabitants in ye Parrish
of Christ Church" in Barbados, contains the
following names: John Hudlice, tailor,
shipped from Southampton on the Virginia,
Captain John Weare; Edward Marsan, "has 10
acres and 6 negroes," and Anthony Slany,
"has 2 negroes."

1735   John Wesley, still an Anglican preacher,
sailed to America on the same ship with the
Moravian Brethren, who influenced him to a
large degree to found the Methodist Church.

The Unitas Fratrum - Unity of Brethren - were
followers of the Czech Hussite Petr Chelčicky;
exiled after 1620, they founded Ochranov
(Herrnhut) in Saxony. This group in a century became overwhelmingly German, but kept
the name Moravian Brethren as a designation
of their origin. Their names testify of
their provenance: Boenisch - Beneš, Boschena
- Božena, Jerschabek - Jeřábek, Lawatsch -
Hlaváč, Watscheck - Vašek, etc. They sent
out missionaries to Greenland, Labrador
("among the Esquimaux"), the Caribbean, and
in 1735 to Georgia, where they received 500
acres from Oglethorpe and preached to the
Creek Indians.

1736   Their bishop David Nitchman arrived in Georgia; he had been ordained by Komenský's
grandson, Daniel Jablonský. A church was
built in Georgia, its minister Anton Seiffert,
Czech by birth.

The first Moravian Brethren appeared in New
York.

1740-1741   11 Brethren from Georgia went to Pennsylvania;
more followed; they founded Nazareth, Beth-
lehem and Lititz (Lidice).

1742   Following Komenský's statement that "no reason can be shown why the female sex . . .
should be kept from a knowledge of language
and wisdom," they founded the first interde-
nominational college for women at Bethlehem.
This town also became a center for church

and classical music and for the art of manu-
script illuminations.

1748   The first Moravian church was built in New
York.

1753   The Brethren were established in Bethraba,
later in Salem, in North Carolina. From
here and the Pennsylvania centers, they ven-
tured forth as the first Protestant missionaries among the American Indians.

1755   April 22. Samuel Barta, an early pioneer
along the Kennebec River in Massachusetts,
petitioned governor William Shirley for protection against the Indians.

1763   A further Moravian church was erected in New
Dorf on Staten Island.

1776   At the time of the Declaration of Independence, there were over 2,000 Brethren and
their family members in the colonies, 600
in Bethlehem alone.

Czech sources indicate that there were Czechs
fighting in the American ranks during the
Revolution, and that William Paca (1740-1799),
signer of the Declaration of Independence for
Maryland, was a descendant of Czechs settled
on the Herrman lands of Bohemia Manor. The
Italians and the Portuguese also lay claim
to him.

1777   Alexander Barta was among the American prisoners captured by the British.

September 23-24. Several thousand troops
had been bivouacked at Bethlehem. A Cong-
ressional delegation paid a visit; John
Adams mentioned in his diary the sweet music and organ of the Brethren, the equal
numbers of men and women at services; he
thought that the "Womens Heads resembled a
Garden of white Cabbage Heads." The Brethren pleaded for the removal of the troops,
their hospital and the British prisoners, as
they disrupted their society. They were
mortified when Congress considered sitting
in Bethlehem for the duration of the war;
the Brethren emphatically declined the complimentary suggestion. [There are close to
60,000 members in the Moravian Church in
America today.]

1791   John W. Kittera, descendant of the Brethren,
            became a member of Congress for four years;
            later he was U. S. District Attorney from
            the Eastern District of Philadelphia.

1805   There was a small settlement called Moravia
            in New Jersey, which disappeared - unless
            history can bring it to light again.

1815   Jiří Rybář settled in Mississippi. Later he
            moved to Texas and became a Mexican customs
            collector in Galveston as Jorge Fisher.

1816   Antonin Filip Heinrich (1781-1861), considered
            the first American composer, arrived from
            Prague; he lived in Philadelphia, Pittsburg,
            later in Boston and New York. While in Ken-
            tucky (1818-1823), he presented Beethoven's
            First Symphony, the first performance in
            America of any of that master's symphonies.

1827   Karel Postel, a writer and newspaperman,
            moved to Texas.

1832   October 8. Antonín Dignowitý from Kutná Hora
            landed in New York; he was a linguist, in-
            ventor, author, physician and abolitionist,
            who practiced medicine in San Antonio until
            his death in 1875. He was a friend of Sam
            Houston. To inform Americans about the fate
            of the Czechs in Austria, he wrote Bohemia
            under Austrian Despotism in 1857.

1834   Professor M. Karel Hrubý and his wife arrived
            from Nové Sedlo to Baltimore. He did manual
            labor, in five years became an apothecary in
            Dayton, Ohio, before he was employed by Mi-
            ami College in Oxford, Ohio, in 1852, as a
            professor of French and German, the first
            of the long line of Czech professors in
            America.

1836   F. V. Vlasák (Lasak), furrier, settled in
            New York. Through cooperation with John
            Astor, he became one of the few Czech mil-
            lionnaires. He did not associate with the
            other Czechs arriving in the 1840's and 1850's.

            April 21. Musician Bedřich Lemský fought at
            the battle of San Jacinto in Nicholas Lynch's
            Company. He settled in Texas.

June 2. Jan Nepomuk Neumann(1811-1860) arrived in New York from the town of Prachatice,
and was ordained the same month as a Catholic priest in the old St. Patrick Cathedral.
He served in upper New York, later in Maryland and Pennsylvania, where he became the
fourth bishop of Philadelphia in 1852. He
was the founder of the American parochial
school system. He was beatified in 1963 and
canonized in 1977.

1840 Dr. Šimon Polák from Domažlice settled in St.
Louis; he founded an eye and ear clinic and
an institution for the blind.

Several Czech families moved to Texas. With
them was father Bohumír Menzl from Frýdland,
whose knowledge of botany and medicinal herbs
helped the settlers' relations with the Indians.

1843 Jorge Fisher was admitted to the bar in
Houston and became a major in the Texas mi-
litia; he was now George Fisher. At the time
of the California gold-rush, he sailed via
Panama and disappeared in the West.

Until the 1840's few Czechs were inclined to
immigrate, as there was no scarcity of employment. But blighting droughts and failing
potato crops during the 1840's stimulated
more individuals to consider the move to
America, as it is indicated by entries in
the town registers in Bohemia.

1846 Vojtěch Sklíba, aged 12, became the first
Czech settler in Chicago known by name. He
lived with his mother in the town of 14,000
people; he was in the saddle and carriage
trade. He was to lose all his property in
the Chicago fire of 1871.

1847 The first Czech settlement in Texas was established at Catspring in Austin County.
The names of 14 early settlers have been preserved. Soon afterwards, other Czechs settled in Industry, Nelsonville, Bleiberville
and San Felipe, in Fayette, Lavaca and Washington Counties.

Čeněk Paclt, "a rolling stone and globe-trot-
ter," was the only known Czech serving in

the Mexican War; he marched triumphantly into Mexico City. After his discharge, he took
off for other ends of the earth and died in
Zululand.

September 16. Karel Havlíček, poet and pat-
riot, whose Pražské noviny was a symbolic
voice of awakening nationalism, admonished
his compatriots not to emigrate. Other papers in Bohemia and Moravia sounded a similar note. But at the same time the daily
press carried advertisements for guidebooks
to America, and the shipping companies vied
for transatlantic passengers, especially for
the "immigrant ships."

Czech nationals did not cherish being drafted
into the Austrian army. Their resentment
frequently led to desertions. In 1847 39
men of the 35th Pilsen Regiment escaped to
America from the Mainz fortress. Among them
was Tůma, the general's orderly, who became
the first correspondent to the homeland papers, extolling life in America. He owned
what he called the "Czech Casino" in New
York. He was nicknamed "the Czech Columbus"
because of his early arrival. Many followed
his example; a military accountant, Toužimský,
"patriotically" fled with the regimental
funds.

1848   After the failure of the 1848 revolution,
many "forty-eighters," fearing reprisals,
immigrated to America. The exodus of musicians, tailors, cabinet-makers. watch-makers,
engravers, brewers, farmers, laborers and students was heading toward the shores of freedom.

December. Vojta Náprstek, a law student,
arrived in New York to avoid imprisonment by
the Austrian government. His nationalism
was in the old Hussite tradition: to question and to challenge any ideology. He
transplanted to American soil the ideas of
Karel Havlíček, the Czech Sam Adams, and embarked on a brief editorial career that took
him to Milwaukee and subsequently to most
Czech settlements in the United States. He
was also an early exponent of the freethinker
movement. In his footsteps, cultivating the
small seed into a wide-branched tree, came
later freethinkers, the editors Ladimír
Klácel, F. B. Zdrůbek, Václav Šnajdr and
countless others...

Among the "48-ers" was Philip Bruckman, the physician; August Hubáček, the popular saloon keeper; his brother John, sexton of the Methodist Church, who introduced prune trees to Rochester, N.Y.; Wenzel Tvrdý, the tailor and furrier from Roudnice, whose son became the first American baby of Czech parents, and numerous other shoemakers, musicians, toymakers, weavers, jewelers, cabinet-makers, etc.

Also in 1848 came Max Mareček (1821-1890), composer and conductor of the Astor Place Opera House in New York; he wrote two autobiographical sketches: <u>Crochets</u> <u>and</u> <u>Quavers</u> and <u>Sharps</u> <u>and</u> <u>Flats</u>.

Franc V. Červený was not a victim of politics, but an able businessman, sent to America as a representative of the family business in musical instruments. He arrived on the same ship with Náprstek and later moved to Milwaukee, where in 1858 he started manufacturing musical instruments.

This year saw the first Czech settlers in Cleveland, later to become one of the largest Czech centers. Gustav Adam, a political refugee, was a musician and long associated with the Cleveland Atheneum. He was followed by three Jewish compatriots, L. Levy, B. Weidenthal and Z. Stein.

The earliest important Czech rural settlements in America were established in Wisconsin. The first Czech arrived in Milwaukee, but the first farming town was Caledonia, north of Racine, referred to as the Bohemian Bethlehem. Many came on foot, carrying feather beds and a few pots; a little girl hugged a kitten in her arms. These Czech tillers of the soil were producing corn, wheat, potatoes, maple sugar and dairy products. To cover cash expenses, they were felling trees. They centered in the counties of Manitowok, Kewaunee, Oconto, LaCrosse, Adams, Marathon and a few others. Their hamlets bore names like Mělník, Krok, Pilsen, Slovan and Tábor. The stream of westward settlers would be fed from here, as well as from new arrivals at the eastern ports, moving in later years to Iowa, Kansas, Nebraska and some to Texas.

In this Wisconsin of the Germans, Norwegians,
Irish and Czechs, the daily wages were 75¢
and board, or $1 without board; skilled car-
penters drew $1.50; domestics received $1.75
per week.

1849   Larger numbers arrived in the aftermath of
1848; some were colorful characters and some
highly community minded individuals. Fran-
tisek Korbel, a university student of engi-
neering, crossed the border disguised as a
woman to escape the warrant for his arrest;
he started out as a cigar maker in New York,
from there went on to manufacture cigar boxes;
he acquired redwood forests and established
vineyards in Sonoma, California. Through a
bureaucratic oversight or impressed by his
richess, Austria appointed him consul in
San Francisco.

The tailor Jaeger came in 1849 from Kutná
Hora; he became the father of the concert
violinist and abbot of the Czech St. Prokop's
Abbey at Lisle near Chicago.

Tomáš Juránek, the apostate priest, as he
described himself, became a cigar maker and
later moved to Wisconsin; John Konvalinka
became a known furrier in Maiden Lane of New
York (his son would become a doctor); Josef
Kriklava turned from college student to pho-
tographer and wine merchant. Václav Pohl of
Pilsen, woodcarver and cabinet-maker, fought
on the barricades of Prague in 1848; in
America, he first opened a grocery in St.
Louis with his wife and brother, but soon
was keeping a tavern in Milwaukee, then farming in Kewaunee. He was a great organizer
of fraternal lodges.

The California goldrush attracted adventurous individuals, but no Czech groups are
known to have set out to "get rich quick,"
nor did permanent Czech settlements arise
on the Pacific coast. Because of slow com-
munications and the long distance from sea-
ports, the news about the "nuggets of gold
ore weighing a pound or more" was reflected
in immigration figures only 3-4 years later,
and in the case of the Czechs even then the
attraction was more "America" than the gold
fields of the west.

1850   Among the 87 Austrian nationals in Califor-
        nia (of the 946 in the U. S.), half can be
        considered to have been Czechs.

        Further "48-ers" arrived, among them Anton
        Kociǎn of Břeclav with 21 others, and Antonín
        Fiala, whose son became the polar explorer.

        The New York group founded the first Czech
        organization on American soil, the Česko-
        Slovanská Jednota (Czecho-Slavic Union), a
        benevolent and educational society with head-
        quarters in a tavern at 14 City Hall Plaza;
        it lasted two years. Náprstek was instrumen-
        tal in its founding, and became the librari-
        an of the society; Václav Pohl was president.

1851   Dr. František Adolf Valenta practiced medi-
        cine and ran an apothecary shop in Chicago.

1852   Thirty Czech families lived in St. Louis.

        16 families arrived in Cleveland and were
        temporarily sheltered in the home of L. Levy.

        The first settlers started arriving in Iowa
        by ox team from Racine and Caledonia in Wis-
        consin, settling on the banks of the Iowa
        river in Johnson county. Many of them were
        from the Pilsen region; among them was the
        baker Drbohlav in Cedar Rapids.

        April 1. Vojta Náprstek started in Milwau-
        kee the weekly Milwaukeer Flugblaetter (Mil-
        waukee Flyleaves)"For Truth and Fun"; as
        there were few prospective Czech subscribers,
        it was published in German, marked "Published
        by a Czech." During its two years of exis-
        tence, there were 250 Czech families in and
        around Milwaukee, some getting on well, es-
        tablishing a brewery, a cheese processing
        plant and a brick factory; nevertheless, this
        was not a sufficient number to support a
        newspaper; thus the only Czech periodical
        published in America in German folded on
        April 29, 1854.

        In Chicago, the first settlers were squatters
        at the site of the present Lincoln Park.
        They did manual labor, cutting trees and
        loading lumber, much in demand for the build-
        ing of houses and sidewalks. Among these
        Chicago pioneers was Anna Dolejšová from

Orlík, who lost two children on the crossing
and later her husband in the Civil War; the
members of weaver Josef Kolář's first Czech
musical band; the former mayor of Kestřany
with wife and seven children, one of whom
became the first Czech nun in America and
taught at the St. Wenceslas school attached
to the church of the same name; Josef Fišer,
the baker, who after a checkered career settled down with his third wife and 13 children and run a popular Immigrants' House and
inn until 1870.

In the winter the ship <u>Amor</u> arrived in Boston with a small group of Czech immigrants.
Among these was František Kořízek (1820-1899),
a mason from Letovice, and as so many other
tradesmen, also a musician. Inspired by
reading about Benjamin Franklin, he decided
to become a publisher; he would cover his
losses by extra income as a musician. Kořízek
became the Nestor of Czech journalism in
America. His daughter Christina married
Charles Jonáš, the other, Cecilia, Václav
Šnajdr, both well known liberal editors.
Another passenger on the <u>Amor</u>, John Bárta,
edited the <u>Slowan</u> <u>Americký</u> in Iowa City in
1869. None of the <u>Amor</u> passengers are known
to have remained in Boston.

1854   In Texas, 12 Czech families settled in Fayetteville, 11 in Praha, others in Bluff,
Dubina, Roznov and Ammansville.

In Iowa, Václav Riegl purchased 20 acres of
land in Linn county for $ 100; a century la-
ter he would have paid $ 250 for one acre.

Josef Francl was the first Czech known by
name to have crossed the continent to California, hardly suspecting that he traversed
dozens of counties, where Czech settlements
would spring up during his lifetime. After
three years, but without gold, he settled as
a piano teacher in Watertown, Wisconsin. Later he opened a store outfitting emigrants
for the west in Crete, Nebraska. He answered
the call of the wild once more and died on
his way west in 1875 near Fort Klamath, where
he was buried.

In the oldest Czech colony, New York, there
were about 40 families by now. Francis

Brodský had returned after a whaling expedition, one of the few of his compatriots who
tried life at sea.

In St. Louis that year the first Czech Catholic church in America was built, dedicated
to the Czech saint Jan Nepomucký. Its priest
was Jindřich Lipovský of Lipovice, son of
the noble family, who had arrived four years
earlier and had been ordained at the Coron-
delet Seminary. The following year a school
was opened at the church, with František
Pešek as first teacher.

Things were looking up in St. Louis, when an
immigrant advertised to "trade 40 acres . . .
for a good piano." The Czechs made one of
their most important moves that year in St.
Louis:

March 4. Four months before the founding of
the Republican Party at Ripon, Wisconsin, at
the initiative of Hynek Vodička of Pilsen, a
"48-er" college student now butcher, they
founded the Česko-Slovanská Podporující Spo-
lečnost (Czecho-Slavic Benevolent Society),
Č.S.P.S. for short. It is the oldest conti-
nuous benevolent organization in the U. S.
The members were simple folk, laborers,
tradesmen, artisans, innkeepers. During
their first meetings, they sat on bags of
hops at Jakub Mottl's saloon; dissenting
Catholics were bodily ejected from the founding meeting.

This non-profit fraternal insurance organization charged 50¢ a month; it paid $ 2 per
week in case of sickness, $20 toward funer-
al expenses (only $ 10 for wives' funerals)
and $ 5 monthly to widows. The by-laws of
the Č.S.P.S. became the first printed Czech
publication in America. The St. Louis Č.S.P.S.
became the nucleus upon which hundreds of future lodges were patterned.

Aside from insurance and aid to new immigrants,
the Č.S.P.S. activities branched out to cultural and educational enterprises, theatrical and choral groups, supplementary schools
and the building of National Halls. Social
programs helped keep youth off the streets,
thus lessening the chances for juvenile de-
linquency. Support of orphans and old peo-

ple eased the burden of the few existing public social services at a time when there were
no social security or pension programs. The
lodges encouraged adjustment to the American
way of life and ownership of homes, thus con-
tributing to solid citizenship. In time,
English speaking lodges were founded within
the Č.S.P.S., thus preserving membership
through several generations both for insurance and for a continuum of ethnic cultural
awareness.

September 28. In Spillville, Iowa, the first
Catholic mass was offered in the home of Jan
Dostál.

1855   In St. Louis the first Czech Protestant <u>Pray-
er Book</u> in America was published by Dr.
Mossock.

In Fayetteville, Texas, the reverend Joseph
Zvolánek held the first Czech evangelical
services.

Ten Czech families lived in Buffalo, New
York, but except for the Myškas, all soon
moved elsewhere.

In Chicago, with fewer than 100 Czechs, Jan
Slavík's tavern opened, proudly displaying
on its marquee "Česká hospoda." It included
a dance hall. The reason for so many early
taverns was not merely the Czechs' predilection for beer; no English was needed to ca-
ter to the "krajané"; furthermore, the breweries supplied the initial investment. Many
a musician found himself tavern keeper in
America.

The new settlers near Traverse City, Michigan, almost starved during their first winter,
except for flocks of wild pigeons. Later
settlements were at Karlín, Maple City, Meno-
minee, Suttons Bay, Swartz Creek, etc.

During this and the next year, Czechs followed Germans and Scandinavians to Minnesota
Territory. They lived near Owatonna, Chat-
field and Hopkins, where their raspberry cul-
tivation was flourishing. Emigrants from
Iowa founded New Prague, which in a few years
grew to 2,000 inhabitants. With the Germans,
they erected a Catholic church, where Peter

Malý was their pastor. His cousin Josef ministered to about two dozen Wisconsin communities. The Minnesota Czech settlers were mostly Catholic, only about 15% freethinkers; these often joined a church after they married a believer. From New Prague the Czechs spread to other centers, founded Veselý, Lytomyšl, Morava, Bechyně, Beroun, Komenský and others. Not until 1883 did they build their own church of St. Wenceslas.

March 5. Bohemia on Long Island, N.Y. was founded by the families of Josef Koula, Jan Kratochvil and Jan Vávra. This was one of the rare Czech agricultural communities in New York State. Called originally Tábor after the Hussite encampment, it had about a dozen Czech families by the end of the decade.

1856   In New York the first school teaching Czech language and history was opened.

In Kossuthtown, Wisconsin the first Czech play was produced by an amateur group. In the same year the Czechs participated in their first political rally, this one for John C. Frémont, who on the new Republican ticket gave Democrat James Buchanan a stiff race for the presidency in most of the 31 states of the Union.

Charles Čulek became the first permanent settler in Nebraska Territory. He lived near Humboldt and carried his supplies 75 miles from St. Joseph.

1857   Libor A. Schlesinger, another "48-er," originally from Chrudim, migrated from Cedar Rapids, Iowa, to Nebraska, establishing his homestead near the Omaha Indian Reservation. In his native land he was a member of the Bohemian Diet; here he was a teamster, transporting goods between Omaha and Denver.

John Koula from Mnichovice, an early resident of Bohemia, N.Y., moved to Boston and subsequently to New Bedford.

Cleveland received its priest, father Anton Krásný, who had been incarcerated since 1849, but under the amnesty of this year was allowed to emigrate.

As a result of the same amnesty, Vojta Náprstek returned to Prague, where he devoted the rest of his life to familiarizing his countrymen with America. He founded an American Museum; a club of American women met at his house, which was the meeting ground for all American Czechs visiting the old country.

May 16. The Č.S.P.S. in St. Louis organized the first grand parade, with music and speeches and all the appurtenances.

As part of the national renaissance, the Czechs in Prague had established in 1848 a patriotic and cultural organization called the Slovanská Lípa (Slavic Linden). In 1857 the first such association on American soil was born in Detroit. Within the next dozen years every larger Czech center had a Slovanská Lípa, organizing theatricals, choirs, libraries, lectures, night schools and other cultural and social functions.

1858   The Protestants established their church in Ely, Iowa; their pastor was the reverend Francis Kún, a Hungarian missionary.

1859   St. Louis established its Slovanská Lípa, a Czech library, and in the fall produced the comedy "One of Us Has to Get Married."

Joseph Horský with his sons in a covered wagon followed the slogan "Pike's Peak or Bust" in the gold-rush. They settled in Nebraska and later in Montana.

Czechs were arriving in Texas mostly through Galveston. Without tools and stock, their beginnings form a special chapter of American frontier history, from dirt cabin to respectability, from early pioneers to B. P. Matocha, Secretary of State of Texas. Their first school was at Wesley in Washington county; teacher Josef Mašík, the first professional Czech teacher in America, held classes in the Protestant church. Some of the Czech schools eventually became parts of the Texan state system, retaining their Czech names until today. Numerically, the Catholics were in the majority among Texan Czechs; they established a church in this year, but did not get a priest until 1872, when Josef Chromčik came. The Catholics established their own schools.

The number of Czechs in the United States by
the end of the 1850's was nearing 10,000.
Most were laborers, skilled tradesmen and
artisans, with a handful of professionals
and intellectuals among them. The farmers
came from the middle class of farmers, as
the rich did not care to leave their lands,
and the poor could not finance the voyage.
First it seemed that St. Louis would become
the largest Czech center in America, conveniently accessible by water. But when Chicago was connected with the east by rail after
1853, it was easier and cheaper to reach.
Thus Chicago took over the lead to become
the second largest Czech city after Prague.
New York and Cleveland were becoming also
Czech urban centers, while Czechs as a group
soon disappeared from New Orleans, Buffalo
and Dubuque, due to removal or assimilation.
Agricultural settlements of the Czechs were
spreading westward from Wisconsin, and the
group in Texas was growing. After the initial hardships of the 1850's, several groups
could turn to less tangible concerns, and
the next decade would witness, aside from
educational and other cultural activities,
a remarkable initiative for newspapers and
magazines, not necessarily successful ones,
but indicating interest for communication
and for the better things of life.

1860   January 1. On a $ 40 press, for which he
            had to mortgage his cottage, František
            Kořízek, the mason and musician inspired by
            Franklin, started publishing in Racine the
            first Czech newspaper on the continent, the
            Slowan Amerikánský (American Slav). It was
            a semi-monthly, then a weekly, with about
            450 subscribers. The frequent appearance of
            the word "Slav" in 19th century Czech publi-
            cations reflects the temporary hopes of Czech
            nationalists looking toward the Slavic breth-
            ren in Russia for support against Austrian
            supremacy.

            January 21. The weekly, Národní noviny (Na
            tional Newspaper) was launched in St. Louis,
            edited by Jan B. Erben, later founder of the
            American Sokol.

October 16. The Lincoln Rifle Company was
formed by 50 Czech volunteers; it was the
first Chicago company to move out from the
city to the front six months later. P. Hudek
was captain, A. Uher first sergeant. Lt.
Colonel G. Michaloczy fell at Buzzard Roost,
Tennessee. Frank Přibramský went through 38
battles unhurt.

The composer Jan Balatka became the dirigent
of the Philharmonic Society of Chicago.

1861   October 30. The two struggling newspapers
merged under the name Slávie (Slavia), published in Racine, the town which by now had
a Slovanská Lípa, a Czech school and library.
The Slávie marked the beginning of extensive
publication activities, mostly by liberals
and freethinkers. Slávie had a number of
distinguished editors, among them František
Mráček (who became involved in the somewhat
visionary efforts of resettling Czech immigrants from the United States to Asian Russia;
Mráček ended up as the sole resettled person).
He was followed by Vojtěch Mašek, whose business ambitions found the job not challenging
enough; and by Charles Jonáš, the future
Democratic lieutenant governor of Wisconsin.
For close to a century, this paper was to a
large extent the voice of Czech America. It
maintained a neutral posture in matters of
politics and religion, carried national and
international news, devoted a large section
to literature and to information for pros-
pective settlers in the west, often noting
the existence or lack of a library in a new
settlement. It had a message service and
price index for various localities. It also
published books. Southerners seeing this
paper thought it was dealing with slavery;
after having some of the articles translated
and discovering its abolitionist tone, they
threatened the Texan subscribers with mob-
bing. Slávie was published until 1946.

During the Civil War Czech sympathies were
overwhelmingly on the Union side, not only
because more of them lived in the north, but
they were followers of Lincoln and abhorred
slavery. Their newspapers were outspokenly
unionist even in St. Louis, and in Texas Dr.
Dignowity was a strong voice against slavery.
Czechs fought at Chancellorsville, Fredericks-

burg, Bull Run and elsewhere; one was present
at Lee's surrender to Grant. The Iowa 22nd
regiment had a Czech company, as did the Wisconsin 36th. Czechs served in New York's
7th, 8th, 12th, 58th, 75th and 93rd regi-
ments; among their officers here were Jan
Pilsen, K. Říha, Captain L. Kinský and Lt.
Colonel Count Edward C. Wratislav. There
were Czech volunteers in Detroit, Saginaw,
Baltimore, Cleveland and in other towns.
Some served in the Home Guards. The St.
Louis Union volunteers were formed secretly
of 46 men and a 14 year old doctor's orderly,
Antonín Klobása. William E. Boleška was
bandmaster with the Union army (and later
with the Brooklyn Navy Yard), the first of
many conductors in uniform who were to dot
the map of the U. S. forces from Annapolis
to Guam in the future. As one Czech historian commented: there were more Czech musicians than generals in the Civil War.

1862   Sixty Czechs and some Germans marched from
Texas to enlist in the Union army, but were
massacred on the Nueces river by Duff's Confederate raiders. The family tragedies of
some Czechs were parallel to those of many
native Americans: in Hostyn, Texas, a monu-
ment indicates that a Czech father fought on
the Confederate side, while his son was in
the Union army.

The Homestead Act was passed, making 160
acres available for a small fee to all who
would work the land for five years. This
law further encouraged Czechs to settle on
the rich farmlands of the Midwest. Nebraska
became the goal of many families, especially
after the railroad reached it at the time
the Civil War ended. Cedar Rapids by now
had 17 Czech families.

Chicago's Czech community reached 500 families; they had the first Czech lawyer, K.
Koláčník. After Racine, Milwaukee and
Cleveland, now Chicago's Slovanská Lípa
opened a Czech language school. While the
Catholic parochial schools offered full instruction to pupils, the liberal or freethinker schools were mostly only language
schools, offering also Czech history, usually on Saturdays.

1863   Charles Jonáš took over the editorship of the
        Slávie for the next two decades. He was re-
        spected by friend and foe for keeping reli-
        gious debates out of the paper. He was a
        Democrat, and such was his moral influence
        that the Czech vote followed him. Subsequent-
        ly Jonáš became state senator (1883) and
        lt. governor of Wisconsin (1890), and member
        of the U. S. consular service, serving also
        in Prague.

        February 22. The Slovanská Lípa of Chicago
        put on the first play, the comedy "Pan
        Strýček" ('The Uncle"), the beginning of a
        rich amateur theatrical program of four an-
        nual performances. Many plays were written
        by the immigrant men and women themselves.
        The Lípa circulating library contained 112
        volumes and numerous periodicals printed in
        America and in Prague.

        October 17. The weekly Pozor (Watch) start-
        ed publication; the title was later changed
        to Americký pozor (American Watch); it last-
        ed 4 years.

1864   To facilitate acclimatization to America,
        the Nová škola (New School) was founded in
        Racine to teach English. The first Czech-
        English dictionary was prepared.

        September 17. Chicago inaugurated the Czech
        National Hall with a stage and social rooms,
        with modern gas lighting, proudly flying the
        Czech flag - with reversed colors!

1865   In Chicago the first Catholic church was
        dedicated to St. Wenceslas. Father František
        X. Šulák, sent from Kroměříž started birth,
        marriage and death registers. His natural
        science collection was to become the nucleus
        of the St. Procopius College collections.
        The same year father Josef Hessoun took charge
        of St. Nepomuk chapel in St. Louis and made
        it a stronghold of Czech Catholicism.

        In Racine Charles Jonáš finally acquired the
        Czech diacritic types and published the Bo-
        hemian-English Interpreter, and the first
        original Czech book in America, Charles
        Procházka's Pravda (Truth). F. B. Zdrubek's
        English Grammar soon followed.

February 14. In St. Louis the Sokol (Falcon) gymnastic organization was founded, patterned after the Sokol of Prague (1862). Within a dozen years, there were Sokols in most Czech centers, eventually 120 all over the United States. Because of its program, the Sokol has attracted, more than the other nation-wide organizations Slovanská Lípa and Č.S.P.S., not only Czechs of several generations, but also Americans of other backgrounds. They maintain their own libraries and choirs, and still organize periodical "slets," where hundreds of gymnasts perform in unison to music.

April 14. Lincoln was shot at Ford's Theatre in Washington. The tragedy was mourned by the whole Czech community. Edward Holý left an eyewitness account of the assassination. Delegations from several cities attended the funeral.

December 31. The Slovanská Lípa held the first Czech congress in Chicago, chaired by Charles Jonáš. One side issue was the founding of a Czech colony, not unlike the one Augustine Herrman had dreamed about; but there were insufficient subscribers to the idea.

1866   The first Czech Workmen's Club was founded in Chicago; others followed in Cleveland (1869) and New York (1870).

The end of the Civil War and of the Austro-Prussian War resulted in a larger influx of immigrants. Especially after Austria lifted its ban on emigration, the branch offices of shipping lines in Prague, Klatovy and other Czech towns increased their advertising campaigns for passengers. Most Czech immigrants passed through New York, but not many remained there among the 1,500, living in poor rooming houses around the lower East Side, in Essex, Division, Houston, Delancey and Rivington Streets.

1867   The first Czech settlement was founded in Kansas, at Marak. Later a large center arose at Wilson, where pioneer J. Švehla, county surveyor and judge, advertised in the Czech papers and attracted many settlers.

In Chicago the Association of Czech Brethren
was established, but lasted only until 1881.

September 25. Karel Jonáš established the
freethinkers' Pokrok (Progress), an anti-
clerical weekly for "Progress of education,
nation, liberty." Its editors were Josef
Pastor and F. B. Zdrubek; it moved from Chicago to Racine, Cedar Rapids and finally to
Cleveland, before it expired in 1878.

As a response to Pokrok, father Josef Molitor
of Chicago started the first Catholic weekly,
Katolické noviny (Catholic Newspaper), but it
ceased within one year.

1868   February. Národní noviny (National Newspaper), the second of that name, started publication in St. Louis. It was the first
social-democratic or socialist Czech paper,
antedating by two years the one in Prague.
This weekly was edited by Lev J. Palda, the
father of the Czecho-American workers' movement and a leader in the Czechoslovanic International Workers Club in New York. The
paper could not survive even after trans-
ferred to Chicago and ceased publication in
1871.

July 26. The first of the five major women's
organizations was founded in New York:
Jednota Dcer Vlasty (Union of Vlasta's Daughters). It was affiliated with the Č.S.P.S.

The first Catholic school was established in
Bluff (later renamed Hostyn), Texas, with
Teresie Kubátová as teacher.

An interesting incident was recorded in Bohemia, N.Y. Josef Nohovec and his friends
categorically objected to the display of religious pictures on classroom walls; a judge
and a constable had to intervene and remove
them.

Josef Sládek, the Czech poet, arrived, but
could not stay away from his native roots
for more than two years. He contributed to
ethnic publications, translated Longfellow
and the Constitution.

November. The weekly Slovan Amerikánský

(<u>American</u> <u>Slav</u>) started publication in Iowa City, later in Cedar Rapids. The editor was a recent arrival: 60 year old ex-priest, Fourierist and visionary Ladimír Klácel (1808-1881), who hoped for a Czech "Svojanov" community in the Black Hills of the Dakotas. The weekly existed until 1920.

1870   There were over 40,000 Czechs living in the United States, the largest numbers, in descending order, were in the states of Wisconsin, Illinois, Iowa, Missouri, Minnesota, New York, Michigan, Nebraska, Ohio and Texas; but almost every state or territory had some Czech inhabitants by now. The largest urban concentration was in Chicago and St. Louis, followed by Cleveland, New York and Milwaukee.

When Rockefeller established the Standard Oil Company, his neighbor Josef Kříž declined to become a stockholder in the "dubious venture" and thus missed becoming a rich man. Nevertheless, Standard Oil provided jobs for many Czechs in Cleveland and elsewhere.

The settlements in Dakota Territory were started, not by professional farmers as was the case in Wisconsin, Iowa and Nebraska, but by laborers tired of city life, especially from Chicago. Some of the places where they found new homes were: Žižkov, Tábor, Vodňany, Courtland, Lesterville, Yankton, Bláha, Janoušek, Havlíček, Houdek, Kašpar, Kolda, Planá, Kolín.

The seventies also saw a few Czechs migrating to Pennsylvania, but few were attracted to the mills and mines.

In Chicago, the famous LYRA male and later mixed choir was founded; it still exists.

September 27. The second women's group was started in Cleveland: Jednota českých dam (Union of Czech Ladies); Karolina Rychlíková was the moving force behind it.

December 2. Just a few days after the 250th anniversary of the Battle on the White Mountain, the Jednota svobodomyslných (Union of Freethinkers) was founded and within a few weeks counted 31 branches from New York to Nebraska and from Louisiana to Minnesota.

F. B. Zdrůbek was one of the moving spirits behind it.

1871   The first Czech farms were springing up near Wahpeton, in future North Dakota.

The Chicago tailors organized the Český krejčovský sbor (Czech Tailors' Association).

The Lucerna (Lantern) was the first New York Czech paper; it was handwritten and not surprizingly lasted only one issue.

The settlements in Nebraska were prospering. Omaha was the springboard to the other centers: Wilber, Crete, Weston, Tobias, Schuyler, Clarkson, Niobrara, Praha, Tábor and several others. Farmer Frank Rychtařík was referred to as the "Western King." Edward Rosewater became the first of 48 state legislators in the next five decades (20 Democrats, 16 Republican, 12 other).

September. The first Czech mass in Nebraska was celebrated by the Jesuit father František Šulák near Prague, at the home of farmer Josef Šimánek.

The weekly and later daily Pokrok Západu (Progress of the West) was founded as the organ of the Czech Farmers Mutual Aid Society in Nebraska. It had Republican leanings. It was edited by the respected Jan Rosický (1845-1910). The paper was bought out by the Chicago Denní Hlasatel and folded in 1920.

In the next 50 years about three dozen periodicals were issued in Nebraska, many by Jan Rosický, who also published books, pamphlets, agricultural and legal guides.

1872   January 2. Father Josef Hessoun started the weekly, later semi-weekly Hlas (Voice), the most important organ of the Catholics until the Czech Benedictine Press was established in Chicago. The paper continued until 1950.

February 19. The first issue of the Hlas Jednoty svobodomyslných (Voice of Freethinkers' Union) came off the presses in Iowa City. It was a monthly, published later in Milwaukee, New York and Chicago under editor Ladimír Klácel and lasted until 1881. Czechs

referred to the Catholic and freethinking
Voices jokingly as "kocouři a mnišáci", cats
and mice, but in a play of words the latter
meant both mice and monks [myš - mouse,
mnich - monk].

October 8. The Great Fire destroyed much of
Chicago. Through the ingenuity of a few
Czechs, their neighborhood was relatively
little damaged.

November 15. In Cleveland the first of a
long line of humorous periodicals appeared,
the Diblík (Little Devil), full of puns,
limericks and jokes, indicating that the
seeds of Švejk were sown long before the
Good Soldier slid down from Jaroslav Hašek's
pen into the classical literature of humor.

1873   The first of about two dozen Czech schools
         in Nebraska was founded. Some lasted into
         the 1930's.

         Editor Palda found that 95% of the New York
         Czechs were employed in cigarmaking. Many
         of them came from Sedlec, a Czech town with
         a cigar industry, and soon were joined by
         others. Tailors, butchers, musicians, new-
         comers looking for a job, ended up making
         cigars in New York. Workers lived in com-
         pany housing on the lower East Side along
         Avenue B, called "Czech Boulevard." Palda
         tried to organize a co-operative among them,
         but met with no success.

1874   June 25. Newyorské listy (New York Gazette)
         was launched; after suspensions and changes
         it emerged as a daily New Yorské listy in
         1886 and merged with the Americké listy
         (American Gazette) in 1966 under the latter
         title as a weekly.

1875   May 22. Palda founded the weekly Dělnické
         listy (Workingman's Gazette) in Cleveland.
         Later it moved to New York. It was the first
         of five papers under this title up to 1904.
         Palda claimed it to be the organ of the So-
         cialist Labor Party, founded the previous
         year. Palda was a socialist, who believed
         in change by evolution, rather than revolu-
         tion.

The Knights of Labor had several Czech
branches in the 1870's; in New York, Chicago, Cleveland, LaCrosse, Wisconsin and a
few others.

October 8. August Geringer founded in Chicago the first Czech daily in America, the
Svornost (Concord). It had also the longest
lifespan as a daily, becoming defunct on
May 30, 1957. It upheld the cause of free
discussion and rationalism. Geringer also
published books and pamphlets, i.e. "How
to Become Naturalized?" a Czech-English dic-
tionary and a history of the United States.
Svornost in time published branch issues in
five cities, i.e. Věstník Iowský (Iowa Bulletin) in Cedar Rapids, with local news.

1876   The Česká osada (Czech Colony) that had pre-
viously attempted group migrations to the
west, undertook a plan for a colony in the
southwest. They investigated Shasta county
in California, but after a young member of
the search team was killed by a train, the
"dreams of rest under the orange trees" re-
ceeded.

Bohemia, N.Y. also manufactured cigars; $ 5
was the wage for a 1,000 handmade ones.
Czechs continued in this work, with adjusted
wages, until 1930, when machines replaced
them.

1877   The Independent Order of Odd Fellows formed
its first Czech lodge, to be followed by
three others before the end of the century.

April 11. The Bohemian National Cemetery was
incorporated in Chicago. It eventually com-
prised 126 acres, with several statues and
a Masaryk Memorial Mausoleum.

July 4. Independence day was celebrated in
Milwaukee by establishing the first Wisconsin branch of Č.S.P.S. Soon 8 others followed in that state. The same year the Catholics initiated the Česká římsko-katolická
první ústřední jednota ve Spojených státech
amerických (First Czech Roman Catholic Central Union in the U.S.A.), also a mutual
benefit association, but in spite of its
dignified title soon 21 branches seceded.
A local historian commented about the Czechs

of those years: "They were distinguished
for their jovial temperament and fondness
of music and song. As farmers they were di-
ligent, steady, and ready to put new ideas
into practice." By the end of the 1870's
the bulk of the Czech immigrants to Wisconsin had arrived, a total of 14,000 people.

July 8. Duch času (Spirit of Time), an illustrated weekly voice of the freethinkers,
with a dash of humor and satire, started ap-
pearing in Chicago; it folded around 1948.

October 10. The weekly and later bi-weekly
Dennice novověku (Morning-Star of the New
Era) had its start in Cleveland as the organ of the Č.S.P.S. In spite of some members' objections to its free-thinking tone,
it remained in print until 1917 (?).

1878   Amerikán, národní kalendář (The American, A
            National Calendar) became one of the most
            popular reading matters in Czech households.
            Its 80 volumes are a treasure trove of eth-
            nic history. A. Geringer of the Svornost
            was the publisher. To the regret of many,
            it folded with its mother publication in
            1957. [Sources also refer to it as an al-
            manac.]

            In Chicago, Leo Meilbeck of Čejč, a former
            cabinet maker, self-made-man and employee
            of the Chicago Public Library, was elected
            to the Illinois legislature, supported by
            the socialists, but opposed by the majority
            of the Czechs. He proposed a bill authoriz-
            ing building and loan associations.

1879   January 10. Sokol Americký (American Sokol)
            was launched as the organ of the Sokol or-
            ganizations, in Chicago. This monthly is
            still being published. In the same year the
            several dozens of Sokol units formed a cent-
            ral National Sokol Union with headquarters
            in Chicago.

            February 6. At LaGrange, the first Czech
            weekly of Texas saw the light of the day;
            its name Texan (Texan) was changed seven
            months later to Slovan (Slav), and it had an
            eleven year long career. At Bluff the same
            year the První texaský česko-moravský Podpo-
            rující spolek (First Texan Czecho-Moravian

Benevolent Association) was founded: four
years later it joined the Catholic unit.

March 3. Antonín Novák started publishing
as a monthly, later as a weekly, Domácnost
(Household) in Milwaukee and in Chicago; it
enjoyed sufficient interest to last until
1930.

June 8. What started as a reading and em-
broidering circle, developed into the third
major women's organization, the Česko-
slovanské podporující dámské spolky (Czecho-
Slavic Ladies Benevolent Clubs) in New York.

November 23. The fourth major women's organization was established by Catholic women:
the Česká katolická ústřední jednota žen
amerických (Czech Catholic Central Union of
American Women) in Cleveland.

In this year Tomáš Čapek (1861-1950) arrived
from Strakonice. After graduating from the
University of Michigan and Columbia Law
School, he became a legislator in Nebraska,
then a successful lawyer and banker in New
York. Yet he found time to turn into a
most prolific writer, both in Czech and in
English, and recorded much of the Czech ethnic experience in America. He has over a
dozen major publications to his name, dealing with Czech immigrants. He was also active in ethnic organizations and in the American movement for the liberation of his native
land.

1880   The following phenomena characterized the
Czech elements in America in the 1880's:
1. There was a growing and visible middle
class with a high percentage of home owners,
and the first of several Czech banks opened
in Chicago (1886); fraternal, educational
and social organizations were in full bloom,
and a proliferation of publications on the
upswing.
2. There was an obvious dichotomy between
Catholics and freethinkers.
3. There was wider participation in local
and state politics. Jonáš' election to two
terms as lt. governor of Wisconsin could be
considered a culmination of such ethnic aspirations. Czechs voted Democratic because
they believed that party more sympathetic to

labor.
4. As a reflection of the growing efforts at a national renaissance in Bohemia, in America new and strong pens tried to strengthen ties with the old country. Aside from editorializing, one expression of this was the launching of group excursions to Prague (1885, 1887, 1889).
5. As radical elements were being expelled from Austria-Hungary, many found their way to the United States and strengthened the so far timid left. Socialist editor Palda found new support. Radicals and anarchists clustered around Proletár (The Proletarian), a New York weekly from 1884 to 1886 (?) and the weekly Dělnické listy (Workingman's Gazette), published in New York, Cleveland or Chicago in 1875-1883, in 1887 and again in 1893-1898, in the last instance by the International Labor Union. After the Haymarket riots of 1884, however, they lost much ground, and after the demise of the last mentioned Dělnické listy, they lost their forum.

The number of Czechs in the United States in 1880 stood at 85,361; by the end of this decade it would swell to 118,106.

1881   It was not evident at the time, but an important arrival to Chicago was 15 year old Adolph J. Sabath, a Jewish Czech, who would become a lawyer and first Czech U.S. Congressman, with a distinguished career in Washington from 1907 to 1952, advocating old age pensions, thus anticipating the Social Security system.

The "Tavern to the City of Pilsen" opened on Chicago's Fisk Street and gave the name Pilsen to the whole Czech section of the city; from there and from "Czech California" the Czechs moved to Cicero, Berwyn and later to Riverside. In all these localities street names and store inscriptions bear witness to Czech residents.

Czechs settled in the future North Dakota around Veselí, Písek, Nový Hradec, Běchyn, Conway, Praha, Lomnice, Lidgerwood and Wyndmere.

1882   This was the year considered by many Ameri-

can historians as the dividing line between
the "old" and "new" immigration, placing in
the former group newcomers from northern
and western Europe, generally from countries
with a variant of representative government,
with a high percentage of skilled and liter-
ate people, and of a Protestant faith. The
latter immigrants from southern and eastern
Europe supplied the much desired unskilled
labor for the accelerating industrialization
of America. This theory is debatable, as
can be shown in the case of the Czechs, who
continued coming at the average number of
5,000 annually in the 1880's, suddenly peak-
ing with 11,758 in 1891, after which year
their numbers declined as low as 1,954 in
1897 and gradually increased to 9,577 in
1903 and to the highest 13,554 in 1907. In
spite of their numbers, no significant proportion of this group fit the above description of "new" immigrants. In the same year
the first federal law limiting immigration
was passed, concerning Chinese labor, hence
not affecting the Czechs.

January 15. The United Cigar-Makers of
America started the monthly Pravda (Truth)
in New York, published in Czech and German;
it was of undefinite but short duration.

The New York Sokol purchased Augustin
Hubáček's saloon on Fifth Street, the place
where fifteen years earlier they had founded
their organization, and now transformed it
into the first Czech National Hall, used until they could afford a new Sokol Hall in
1896.

September 8. The history of Chicagské listy
(Chicago Gazette) illuminates well the struggle of a small ethnic paper. It was published by J. V. Matějka and it was succes-
sively a daily, weekly, bi-weekly, then a
daily again. At one time it had also an
evening edition for almost a year. It suspended publication from March, 1883 to July
1884 and finally died on October 28, 1893,
not being able to compete with the larger
Svornost and several out-of-town Czech papers covering special interests.

October 10. After the typesetters at the
Dělnické listy of New York had struck un-

successfully for higher wages, they established the moderate socialist Dělník americký
(American Workman); for business reasons,
however, they changed the name of the paper
to New Yorské listy (mentioned above) in
1886. This was the paper that eventually
merged with the Americké listy in 1966.

1883   The Č.S.P.S. moved their headquarters from
        St. Louis to Chicago, a symbolical recogni-
        tion of that city as the hub of Czech ethnic
        life in the United States.

1884   An uncommon phenomenon was the publication
        in Czech, but in Hamburg, Germany, of a
        monthly called České osady v Americe (Czech
        Settlements in America), which informed pro-
        spective immigrants about the conditions in
        the various Czech centers. It ceased in
        1892.

        After the purge of socialists in Austria,
        many sought refuge in the United States,
        among them Leo Kochman, who found a vehicle
        for the propagation of his ideas first at
        the New York weekly Proletář (The Proletar-
        ian) together with F. J. Hlaváček, and after
        that paper had folded in about two years,
        at the Hlas lidu (Voice of the People),
        where he remained as editor in chief for 25
        years. This New York daily belonged to the
        Bohemian Workingmen's Cooperative Association,
        was launched in 1886, and after changing to
        a weekly three years later, survived until
        1921 under the name Nedělní hlas lidu (Sun-
        day Voice of the People).

        In Chicago the first Methodist church was
        established by František Hrejsa, considered
        the father of Czech Methodism. He came to
        the United States as a follower of the Czech
        Brethren, worked in a furniture factory be-
        fore being ordained as a Methodist minister.

        October 15. In Omaha, Jan Rosický embarked
        on a literary publishing venture, launching
        the Květy Americké (American Flowers), first
        as a monthly, then as a bi-weekly and a week-
        ly. The magazine combined literary efforts
        with reminiscences of Czech pioneer days
        and the discussion of current problems. In
        the span of 32 years, it was published during
        9, namely 1884-1887, 1900-1903 and 1916-1919.

1885   March 2. The Benedictine fathers arrived at Chicago and started ministering to the needs of the Czech Catholics. Their St. Procopius parish became an important center of Catholic activities.

The first large group excursion to the old homeland was undertaken; of the 150 participants 80 came from Chicago. This expedition was referred to as the "theatre ship," as the initiative came from the "theatre trains," organized in Bohemia to attend the new National Theatre in Prague.

November 1. The Bohemian Opera House was solemnly opened at Manitowok, Wisconsin. It was maintained by the Slovanská Lípa and the Sokols, and served not only the purposes of Thalia, but also as a ballroom, assembly hall, gymnasium and lecture hall. One room served as a dispensary of liquid refreshments, and the ladies had a parlor of their own in the building. In 1974 the opera house stood stripped of its glory, mutely awaiting demolition.

December 10. At LaGrange, Texas, Augustin Hajdusek started editing the weekly <u>Svoboda</u> (<u>Liberty</u>), which had a successful run until 1966. Hajdusek was the first Czech admitted to the Texan bar, who became a judge and a member of the Texan legislature.

1886   May 4. The Haymarket riots in Chicago and their aftermath cut into anarchist activities, fed partly by radicals escaped from Austria. Czech leftists preferred the social democratic movement, which gained strength with the immigrants of the following decade.

The Americká matice pro školy v Čechách (American Council for Schools in Bohemia) launched a drive and collected $ 981.50 for the support of schools in the old homeland.

1887   The Redemptorist fathers cared for Czech Catholics in New York, later built the Church of the Virgin Mary of Perpetual Help with a shrine of the Infant Jesus of Prague.

March 2. The Benedictine fathers in Chicago established the College of St. Procopius at Lisle, Illinois, the only Czech institution

of higher learning in America. In the 1970's
the name of the college was changed to Illinois Benedictine College and it became co-
educational. The language of instruction is
English.

April 29. This date marked the end of still
another experiment in publishing, inspired
as much by a true effort to inform immigrants
as by commercial motives: The Montgomery
Star of Minnesota had been issuing a weekly
Czech supplement for several months but had
to discontinue it. Not till 1904 did the
Czechs of that state have their own paper,
the Minnesotské noviny (Minnesota Newspaper),
a supplement to another newspaper, lasting
for ten years.

June 12. In Chicago, the Sunday School meeting of the Methodists was disrupted by a
crowd, allegedly led by a Catholic priest
lamenting "the devil's doings," throwing
stones, sand, lighted sparklers and other
objects, until the minister had to flee
through the back door. The next meetings
were guarded by two policemen. The group
moved to other quarters, which were adjoin-
ing a tavern; the noise filtered through the
wooden partitions. On the other hand, the
customers in the tavern often quieted down
and listened to the preaching on the other
side of the wooden planks. Here the first
Czech kindergarten was established in 1889.

In the early summer, the second excursion to
Prague took place, this time organized by
the Sokols; 300 Czechs participated.

October. Jan Rosický in Omaha started publication of the Knihovna americká (American
Library), a semi-monthly which printed Czech
and translated works in installments; some
of the authors represented were Verne, Dumas,
Arbes and Jirásek.

A few Czechs settled in the region of Petersburg in Virginia, and others at New Bohemia
in Maryland.

1888   A Czech chronicler of the era had claimed
that the "activities of the anarchists consisted only of disrupting all ethnic programs
and of street brawls"; nevertheless, three

Czech anarchists were arrested and tried for
the possession of explosives: Jan Hronek,
František Čapek and František Chleboun. Only one was.convicted.

Ethnic enclaves were considered missionary
territory by some denominations. Thus Dr.
E. A. Adams of Franklin, Massachusetts, was
sent to organize a congregation among the
Chicago Czechs. He was such an "amiable
and tolerant Yankee," that even the freethinkers respected him. He started out with
16 curious souls, and perhaps because he had
learned Czech, soon had a considerable flock,
sufficient to establish a Congregational
Church. In two more years they built their
own Bethlehem Chapel, named after the one in
Prague, where Jan Hus first preached in the
native language in the 14th century.

The son of the adventurous physician, A. F.
Dignowity from Del Rio, Texas, extended an
invitation to Czech groups to settle on the
30,000 acres left to him by his father.
But the Czechs were too individualistic for
a mass migration, preferring to make their
own choices.

1889   All Czech Catholic lodges united in the
           Česká římsko-katolická jednota texaská
           (Czech Roman Catholic Union of Texas), which
           still functions.

           Oberlin College in Ohio introduced the study
           of Czech language and literature into its
           curriculum.

           April 22. In one of the most spectacular
           moments in frontier history, at the famous
           run on Oklahoma land, 12,000 prospective
           settlers rushed to stake out their claim
           to 160 acre homesteads. There is no record
           that Czechs were among the "boomers and
           sooners" squatting on that land, but there
           were about three dozen of them among the
           crowd at high noon that day, when the run
           got under way. They came from Kansas, Neb-
           raska, Iowa and Texas, and several succeeded
           in gaining a foothold there. Czechs set-
           tled in Oklahoma County. Most took up farm-
           ing; among the rest were a tailor, black-
           smith, doctor, seamstress and a violinist;
           still others opened stores. John Hubatka

was appointed to the police force; he eventually became the Chief of Police in Oklahoma City. Here were again frontier conditions; sod blocks formed walls for pri-
mitive homes for a year or two until the
men and their women broke the land and ex-
tracted a harvest. Cotton and wheat were
the chief crops. Yukon was the Czech "capital" of Oklahoma, but Czechs were also in
Oklahoma City, Piedmont, Banner and El Reno.

1890   The fifth major women's organization was
       founded in Cleveland: Česká sesterská pod-
       porující Jednota (Czech Women's Benevolent
       Union). The name of their first lodge was
       "Love of Fatherland"; 77 other lodges sprang
       up, most in Illinois and Ohio, before they
       merged with the Č.S.P.S. in 1948.

       September. A congress of the Czech Labor
       Party in the United States was held in Chi-
       cago.

       In the 1890's, after the passage of the Mc-
       Kinley tariff, Czechs from Žirovnice ar-
       rived in larger numbers and brought with
       them their skills in pearl button making.
       There were 67 Czech owners of pearl button
       making businesses, employing about 1500
       Czech workmen: 40 in New York, others in
       Connecticut, New Jersey and one in Chicago.
       After the war they still represented half
       of all pearl button manufacturing in the
       United States. The largest factory was that
       of B. Schwanda in New York, responsible for
       half of all production.

       The 1890's were also the decade when Czech
       poetry was flourishing in America, repre-
       sented by František Hlaváček, whose epic
       story of the creation went through five edi-
       tions, L. W. Dongres, who wrote under the
       pen name "Just a Man," Jan V. Brož with his
       collection "The Prairie," and Jan Vránek,
       author of "On American Soil." They were fol-
       lowed in the still pre-war era by Jarka
       Košar, Václav Miniberger, Jindřich Ort and
       others. The Czech periodicals were seeded
       with poetry.

1891   In Omaha, Jan Rosický launched still another
       monthly, Hospodář (Husbandman), a successful
       magazine devoted to agriculture.

May 1. From a typographers' strike emerged the Denní hlasatel (Daily Crier), which survived the competition of three other Chicago papers by having the delivery boys collect weekly subscription monies. This is one of the few Czech papers still published as of 1977, with a circulation of 9,000 (before World War II it was as high as 40,000). Its Sunday edition claims 50,000 subscribers.

September. Č.S.P.S. started publishing Organ Bratrstva (Organ of Brotherhood) in Oak Park, Illinois, later in Cleveland; it ceased in 1932.

September. These were the days of Granges, Farmers' Alliances and the Populist Movement. Nebraska was the home of the "prairie avenger, mountain lion, Bryan," Populist crusader. The Czechs joined their ranks with Přítel lidu (Friend of the People), a Populist weekly issued in Wahoo and later in Wilber. This paper was bought out by the Chicago Hlasatel and silenced in 1915.

September 22. When the Shawnee Potawatomie territories in Oklahoma were opened to homesteading, seven Czech families were among the new settlers.

1892　　　The Workingmen's Sokol was established in New York. Among the founders were Aleš Hrdlička, later world-known anthropologist of the Smithsonian Institution, and Gustav Habrman, future Secretary of Education of Czechoslovakia.

September 1. Releases to the American press and universities at the occasion of the 300th anniversary of Komenský's birth gave impetus to the founding of the Czech-American National Committee, the first national organization, which - as its president Palda hoped - would become a clearing house for the dissemination of news about Czech affairs. He also intended to foster commercial and cultural relations between the United States and Bohemia. The momentum of this trend created the first Czech illustrated monthly in English, the Bohemian Voice, printed in Omaha. Tomáš Čapek was its first editor, and Palda, Jonáš, Rosický, Zdrůbek and Šnajdr were supporting it. It had 1500 subscribers, and 1000 free copies were sent to the press and universities. It lasted two years and ceased because of financial difficulties.

1893   Ludvík's theatrical troupe immigrated to Chicago, where for the next 20 years it functioned as a resident company at the Thalia building in Chicago's Czech Pilsen. They also toured other Czech settlements in America.

June-July. Composer Antonín Dvořák, who since the previous year had been director of the National Conservatory of Music in New York, visited the Spillville, Iowa (population 361) home of Josef Kovařík, the viola and violin player of the New York Philharmonic. Here Dvořák composed the American Quartet in F major, op. 96, the String Quintet in E flat major, op. 97, and put the finishing touches on the symphony "From the New World." They show influence of Indian and Negro music, as well as a blending of Czech and American folk tunes.

August 12. This was Bohemian Day at the World's Columbian Exposition, held a year too late for the 400th anniversary of the discovery. Nearly 28 million people visited it; Bohemian day was by consensus one of its highlights. The Sokol exercises were watched by 15,000 spectators. At the music festival both Dvořák and V. I. Hlaváč, the Czech director of the St. Petersburg opera, conducted their own compositions. The Czech orchestra of 114 members was accompanied by a Czech chorus. In the two hour long parade most of the 258 Czech organizations of Chicago marched, about 20,000 strong. All 16 unions were among them, from typographers and musicians to metalworkers and masons.

August 20. Bedřich Smetana's "Prodaná nevěsta" ("Bartered Bride") was performed in Chicago, with F. Hlaváček of the Prague opera singing Kecal.

September 26. The community at Bohemia, N.Y. erected the first statue honoring Jan Hus; allegedly it was also the first statue in this country honoring a foreigner.

1894   Č.S.P.S. celebrated its 40th anniversary.

February 8. The Chicago Benedictine press added to its weekly Katolík (The Catholic), published since the previous July, the daily Národ (Nation), an influential Catholic voice until its demise in 1975. The last issue of Katolík was dated December 19, 1975.

June. Ženské listy (Women's Gazette) was founded in Chicago by Josephina Humpal-Zeman, a leader in the suffragette movement. It was a weekly, then bi-weekly and monthly; in 1947 it became the Hlas jednoty (Voice of Unity), a weekly, then monthly and by 1974 a quarterly.

1895   Anna Nováková, the wife of a tailor, at the age of 31 became the first Czech woman doctor in America; before the century was out, she was followed by Dr. Palečková of Cleveland and Dr. Šmídová of Chicago.

1896   New York's new National Hall was erected as a common venture of several benevolent organizations; it soon included a moving picture theatre. Cost: around $250,000. The Sokols' gymnasium and club house cost $125,000; the Czech Workingmen's Sokol's home was valued at $225,000.

1897   June 24. All Texas units of fraternal lodges joined in the Slovanská Podporující Jednota Státu Texas (Slavic Benevolent Union of the State of Texas); the same year the Catholic women combined forces in the Česko-římsko-katolická Podporující Jednota Žen Texaských (Czech Roman Catholic Union of Texan Women).

July 4. In a second secession from the Č.S.P.S. the Západní Česko-Bratrská Jednota (Western Czech Fraternal Union) was formed in Cedar Rapids, consisting of 37 lodges in Nebraska, Minnesota, Iowa, the Dakotas, Colorado and Kansas.

1900   As the new century opened, the census counted almost 157,000 Czechs living in the United States. A third of them supported themselves by agriculture in the Midwest and in Texas. As they were relatively early arrivals, most of them owned good, fertile lands; the quality of their achievements as farmers had been acknowledged by several state agricultural departments. Even in the farming communities

there was a proportionate number of shop-
keepers, laborers and tradesmen; others
owned manufacturing companies, seldom of
large size. Czech breweries were usually
not as large as the German ones, but the
Czechs succeeded in placing the names Plzeň
and Budějovice (Pilsen, Budweis) on the map.

Of Czechs born abroad 32% were in agriculture; of the second generation, 42%. The
corresponding figures for breadwinners in
other occupations were: unspecified laborers, 14% and 8.1%; tailors: 6.9% and 3.7%;
in building trades, 5.3% and 4 %; in the tobacco industry, 3.2% and 1.3%; merchants, 3%
and 2.3%. Among the second generation there
were more machinists, salesmen and those in
the professional services.

Of the urban centers, Chicago was by far the
largest. Its Directory of Bohemian Merchants,
Traders, and Societies (which was not all
inclusive) listed for this year 322 tailors,
321 saloon keepers, 266 grocers, 147 butchers,
107 shoemakers, 97 milkmen, 84 confectioners
and stationers, 60 insurance brokers, 60 mid-
wives, 58 dress-makers, 51 shops with wood
and coal, 51 cigar makers, 45 physicians,
43 barbers, 43 lawyers, and down the line
19 each of plumbers, blacksmiths and band-
leaders. There were also 22 music conserva-
tories listed. The over 1500 stores and
businesses owned by the Czechs of Chicago
reflect the popular statement among the
Czechs after World War I, that they were the
Yankees of Europe.

The prewar years of the 20th century were
the peak period for the Czech press; 12
dailies and over a dozen weeklies were being
published. Of the dailies 4 were in Chicago,
2 each in New York and Cleveland. The Květy
americké had its rebirth in this year also.

Spravedlnost (Justice), a new weekly of the
social democrats, was founded in Chicago by
F. J. Hlaváček.

As time went on, more Czechs intermarried
with other nationalities. The census of
this year indicates that Czechs marrying
outside their group showed preference for
Germans (11,167), Austrians (3,417), Hungar-

ians (1,183), Poles (1,065), and Canadians
(636). More Czech women married outside
their group than men, in the sample group
12,519 vs. 7,497.

1901   As Lincoln county in Oklahoma was being settled, one community east of Oklahoma City
was named Prague. It had subsequently several Czech mayors. It was a farming community with a lively Sokol group. Although
oil had been discovered later near Prague,
history does not record any Czech oil mil-
lionaire. Some of the lands where the Will
Rogers airport of Oklahoma City is now, used
to belong to Czech farmers.

1902   Two community leaders arrived in America
this year. One was Václav Miniberger of
Písek, a poet, novelist and newspaperman,
for many years connected with the Chicago
Svornost, whose Malát, a novel in verse, and
Songs of the Prairie, poems, were well received.

The other arrival was university professor
Tomáš G. Masaryk, leader of the Realist Party in Bohemia, who made contacts with the
Czechs in America, that would evolve into
close cooperation in the years to come,
leading to the formation of the Czechoslovak
Republic. Masaryk married in 1878 Charlotte
Garrigue of Brooklyn, a music student he had
met in Leipzig, and took her name for his;
this was the origin of the T. G. M. initials.

Matice vyššího vzdělání (Council of Higher
Education) was founded in Cedar Rapids. Its
originator was Bohumil Šimek. W. F. Severa
and the merchants financed its beginnings.
Its aim was to offer interest-free loans to
men and women to facilitate their college
education. In 1924 it moved its headquarters
to Chicago. During its history hundreds of
students received   aid from the Matice, including the refugees. For many years Jan
Micka was its executive secretary.

1903   Explorer Anthony Fiala led the Ziegler expedition to the North Pole; later he accompanied Theodore Roosevelt on his search and
discovery of the Lost River in Brazil.

The first Komenský Club was founded at the

University of Nebraska in Lincoln. Eventually there were 29 of these educational clubs at various colleges and universities throughout the country. The members, students and professors, were interested in the study of Czech history, language and literature, and also in acquainting the public with their culture. The Matice closely cooperated with these clubs.

Boža Umírov sang a program of Czech songs at the White House.

Bedřich Šrahola (1872-1954) from Komná near Uherský Brod settled in Trenton, N. J., and soon 30 families from his village and its vicinity followed. This state attracted many more Slovaks than Czechs.

1904   Cedar Rapids, as well as other Czech centers, offered classes in English and citizenship to facilitate naturalization; this service continued for several decades.

March 4. Č.S.P.S. celebrated its golden anniversary. By now the benevolent association had 196 lodges, 13 great lodges and over 20,000 members.

1905   Prague in Oklahoma was incorporated, and soon had its St. Wenceslas church.

1906   The New York Public Library opened its Webster Branch, and within 15 years contained 15,000 volumes, the largest library of Czech books in America at that time.

The Czech Federation of Socialist Parties of America was founded. It had 600 members in 20 branches; these numbers doubled just before World War I. Interestingly, many poets were among the members.

Rudolf Friml, pianist and composer, arrived as an immigrant. He was Dvorak's pupil. He came with Jan Kubelík, the violinist and father of Rafael Kubelík, the conductor. Friml was to gain fame for his light operas as "Firefly," "High Jinks," "Rose Mary," "If I Were King" and others.

Adolph J. Sabath was elected as representative from Illinois in the U. S. Congress, where he was to remain for 46 years.

1907   The peak year of Czech immigration brought
13,554 newcomers to the United States.

In the congress of freethinkers in Chicago,
they established the Svaz svobodomyslných
(Rationalist Federation); they referred to
themselves as "religious independents." Dr.
J. S. Vojan was the chief spokesman.

Tomáš G. Masaryk gave a series of lectures
at the University of Chicago on 'The History
of Small Nations," and spoke at Czech ethnic
gatherings about the status of the Czechs in
the Austro-Hungarian empire; his emphasis
was on self-determination.

The first chair of Czech Language and Literature was established at the University of
Nebraska, held by Jeffrey D. Hrbek, born in
Cedar Rapids. After his untimely death, his
sister, Šárka B. Hrbková, took over until 1919,
when the program was cancelled. At various
times similar programs existed at the Universities of Texas, California, Iowa and
Wisconsin, Columbia University, the University of Chicago, Coe and Dubuque College in
Iowa, St. Procopius College in Illinois, at
Oberlin College, at several colleges in Texas and in other states.

1908   Victor H. Duras, born in Wilber, Nebraska,
became the youngest U. S. judge, serving in
Panama. In his later career he was an international lawyer in Washington, D. C. and
the author of treatises in international affairs.

1909   Palda's efforts of 15 years earlier material-
ized with the founding in Chicago of the
Česko-Americká Tisková Kancelár (Czecho-
American Press Bureau) under Dr. J. S. Vojan.
It gathered and disseminated news and information about the Czechs' history, culture
and aspirations. Lectures and film presen-
tations were part of the program. This time
the finances were provided partly through
the generosity of František Korbel, the early
immigrant who became prosperous in California.
Again by a strange coincidence, the man whom
Austria appointed as its consul, contributed
to an organization whose attitude was antag-

onistic to that regime.

The Metropolitan Opera in New York presented
the "Bartered Bride" by Bedřich Smetana.

1910   The slightly over half million first and
            second generation Czechs lived at the begin-
            ning of the second decade of the century,
            with the exception of New York and Texas,
            still mostly in the Middle West, half of them
            in small towns. There were 725 cities and
            towns with more than a hundred Czechs resid-
            ing in them: 154 in Texas, 145 in Wisconsin,
            91 in Nebraska. The states with most Czechs
            were Illinois with 124,225, Nebraska and Ohio
            each with 50,000, New York with 47,000.
            There were Czechs in every state of the Union
            and the two territories. The smallest num-
            ber, 16, was recorded for North Carolina.
            Within the end of the decade two thirds
            would live in urban areas and only one third
            in rural ones; however, that shift would be
            caused not only by the move of the Czech
            population but also by the changes in rural
            America; the trend of the Czechs correspond-
            ed with the overall American trends toward
            urbanization.

            During the fifty years of the Czech press in
            America, 339 periodicals were launched, of
            which 90 were still in existence in 1910.
            They were Catholic, Protestant and free-
            thinker oriented; some managed to stay free
            of the religious aspects; politically they
            were right or left of the center, some were
            socialist. They were local or national in
            scope, geared to selected audiences like labor
            farmers, women or children, or specialized
            in literature, health, Sokol, forestry or
            humor.

            The community as a whole seemed to thrive.
            In New York Tomáš Čapek with four partners
            founded the Bank of Europe. In Chicago, of
            the 197 building and loan associations 94
            were controlled by $ 9 million of Czech capi-
            tal. In the five years following 1910, 69
            new Czech schools enrolled 5,300 children.

            Dr. John Habenicht, the Chicago physician,
            amateur actor and lover of Shakespeare, pub-
            lished his Dějiny Čechův Amerických (History
            of American Czechs), a goodly collection of

reminiscences gathered during his residences in
about a dozen cities from Maryland to Texas.

Dr. Aleš Hrdlička (1869-1943) became the cura-
tor of the Smithsonian Institution in Washington, D. C. He arrived in America in 1882, received a medical education, and gained international reputation in anthropology, especially
in the migration tracks of the American Indians.
He founded the American Journal of Physical
Anthropology and the American Association of
Physical Anthropologists.

In a further effort to coordinate the various
activities of the Czechs in America, the Česko-
Americká Národní rada (Czecho-American National
Council) was established. The explorer, lec-
turer and writer E. St. Vráz was the man in
charge.

December. The Rationalist Federation launched
an illustrated monthly in New York, the Věk
Rozumu (Age of Reason), later moved it to Chicago, where it continued as a weekly.

1911   Tomáš Čapek tabulated crimes among the Czechs
in Chicago, basing his study on city reports.
He found that the Czechs and Russians had committed the smallest percentage of homicides; in
general the Czechs committed fewer offenses of
personal violence and were guilty of a relatively higher percentage of burglaries, equalling
the Canadians and Germans. The Czechs, as well
as the Poles, Canadians, Danes, Germans, Lithu-
anians and Austrians, all exceeded the white
Americans in the number of arrests for disorder-
ly conduct. On the other hand, Czechs became
less frequently public charges or charity cases,
because of the wide-spread provisions for health
and life insurance, and because they took care
of their orphans and old folks.

1913   With a large farming population, there could be
no wonder that a monthly like Drůbežnické listy
(Poultry Gazette), published in Benson, Nebraska, could find readers for five years.

1914   June 28 - July 28. The news that concerned
the average American of the pre-war era had
to do with motor cars, moving pictures, trust-
busting and the Hepburn Act. As to foreign
news - the Panama Canal was about to open.
Reports about Balkan wars were so frequent
that the public got used to them. Thus it
came as a surprise to most Americans

when a shot at Sarajevo ignited the European
powder keg, simmering with the explosives of
economic rivalries, strife for the balance
of power and age old hatreds. Within a month
over a dozen declarations of war were cere-
moniously exchanged, and the carnage began.
Americans were relieved to hear President
Wilson's proclamation of neutrality.

July 28. Even the best among the Czechs in
America knew that they could not comply with
their president's request for impartiality
"in thought as well as in action." With
Austria-Hungary at war with Britain, France
and Russia, hopes were raised for independence from the Hapsburgs. On July 28, the
day Austria declared war on Serbia, a mass
meeting was held at Chicago's Pilsen Park,
demonstrating sympathies with the Serbs.
Slogans like "To hell with Austria" spoke
more clearly than the speeches, and were duly
reported in the American press. Similar
meetings were held in New York, Cleveland,
St. Louis and Baltimore. From sympathies
for the Serbs, the voices soon turned toward
the liberation of the Czech homelands.

August. In the Orgán Bratrstva, the voice
of the Č.S.P.S., editor J. S. Vojan wrote a
rousing article "All Aboard," sounding the
hope that an Allied victory would redraw the
map of Europe.

August 12. Osvěta Americká (American Enlight-
enment) of Omaha carried Jan Janák's editorial expressing hope for Czech independence:
"It is up to us living outside Austria to
take the first step, to be ready to send our
representatives to the governments of Russia,
England and France. . . . We shall need
money." This was the beginning of the Czech
resistance movement against Austria, sounded
from the prairies of the west. The $ 5 and
$ 10 contributions started coming in for the
"Czech Fund."

August 19. Janák continued his editorial
with admirable conviction: "It is certain
that after this war there will be no Austria.
The victorious powers will decide the fate
of its component parts, including Bohemia.
Our compatriots abroad are powerless. The
time has come for us, Czechs overseas, whose

hands are not tied, to communicate our national aspirations to the powers who will
dictate the conditions of the peace. But
they must know what we want." From Kolin
in Louisiana, Oklahoma City, Wilber in Nebraska and elsewhere the dollars kept rolling
in,many with touching messages.

August 27. In New York the Czechs formed
a Czecho-American Committee for Independence
and Support of the Czech Nation, and proclaimed that "all conscious American Czechs
labored for independence of the lands of
the Czech crown," and signed it with "Long
live Czech Independence." They also started
a collection.

September 2. The most important step was
taken in Chicago, when the České národní
sdružení (Czech National Alliance) was
formed by the representatives of the fraternal organizations of Č.S.P.S., Sokols, the
Czecho-American National Council and the
Czecho-American Press Bureau; the socialists
joined in 1915. This Czech National Alliance
was the center of activites and the financial source for the first years of the struggle to liberate the old homeland. Dr.
Ludvík J. Fisher, the Chicago physician,
was the chairman of the Alliance, which by
the end of the war was a well organized network of 320 chapters in 16 regions. Considering their small numbers, the Czech and
later the Slovak ethnic group in America
generated a titanic and unprecedented effort
toward the liberation of their ancestral homelands.

September 13. Emanuel V. Voska and his
daughter Villa returned from a visit to
Prague stopping in London to deliver con-
cealed documents and secret messages from
Masaryk and the Czech patriots to British
intelligence. Voska was a Czech immigrant
self-made man who owned a stone-cutter firm
at Astoria, N.Y. He became one of the most
valuable Allied agents in America. From the
ranks of Czech immigrants he organized a
courier service, employing several women
(Anna Chaloupková and Míla Jarušková of New
York, Marie Kvíčalová of Boston and others).
He set up an 80 member network of Czech immigrants, employed at Austrian and German

shipping lines, businesses, consulates and
embassies. The Czech mail clerk of the
Austrian consulate in New York regularly delivered the mail to Voska to be photographed.
The personal maid of German ambassador Berns-
torff's wife was in his services, as was
the governess at the home of a widow Berns-
torff often visited. The German embassy
chauffeur and an operator at the Sayville
wireless station that cleared German cables
were among his volunteers. Voska's operatives
set up the meeting and wired the room at the
Manhattan Hotel in New York, where the Germans started their conspiracy with the Mexican Huerta, eventually leading to the in-
famous Zimmermann Telegram. They revealed
that Germans were shipping arms to Mexico
in coffins and oil tankers. Voska closely
cooperated with the Alliance. In 1940 he
published his memoirs.

October. Slovak immigrants have been arriving in America since the 1880's; many were
employed in Pennsylvania mines. The Slovaks
had been under Hungarian rule for almost a
thousand years, deprived of a chance for full
national and cultural development. In 1907
in Pittsburgh, the Slovak immigrants joined
in the Slovak League, which expressed a hope
for autonomy under Hungary. In October 1914
its chairman, Albert Mamatey, wrote in the
Chicago Svornost that the best solution for
the Slovaks would be a United States of Bohemia, Moravia and Slovakia, the first ut-
terance that eventually led to the Pittsburgh
agreement between the Czechs and Slovaks to
form a republic together.

November 4. The Czechs dispatched a Red
Cross unit of doctors and nurses to aid the
Serbians. A Voska operative was among them.

1915   May 29. Ground was broken in Chicago for a
            Czech orphanage.

            July 4-6. The Czech community used the com-
            memoration of the 500th anniversary of Jan
            Hus' martyrdom to voice their political de-
            mands for freedom of their ancestral home.
            From freemasons' lodges in San Francisco to
            women's clubs in New York the cause was being
            propagated. Lt. Governor G. D. Cushing spoke
            at Boston's historic Faneuil Hall; prominent

personalities were engaged at rallies in
other cities and towns.

July 24. The excursion boat <u>Eastland</u> cap-
sized at the pier in the Chicago river, and
among the hundreds of lives lost were those
of 249 Czechs, most of them employees of the
Western Electric Company on their annual
outing. For the Czechs it was a disaster
worse than the Chicago fire.

September 23. A momentous series of confer-
ences started in Cleveland between the Alliance and the Slovak League that culminated
in October in the Cleveland Agreement between the Czechs and the Slovaks to cooperate
for a common goal.

1916   Albín Polášek became head of the Department
of Sculpture at the Chicago Art Institute.
His work is displayed in museums throughout
the United States (i.e. "Fantasy" at the
Metropolitan Museum). After the war he was
commissioned by the Alliance to sculpt the
statue of Woodrow Wilson, a gift for the city of Prague, that graced an avenue named
after the president.

In New York the women's Christmas bazaar
yielded $ 22,250 for the cause. In the next
months similar enterprises brought $ 25,000
from Cleveland, $ 40,000 from Chicago,
$ 65,000 from Omaha, $ 55,000 from Taylor,
Texas, and $ 25,000 from Cedar Rapids, Iowa,
etc. By 1918 nationwide offerings added up
to $ 320.000, gathered from donations and
social affairs, bazaars, the sale of badges,
lapel pins and posters. Masaryk acknowledged
a total of $ 674,885 as the contribution of
his American compatriots between the Fall of
1914 and May 1918.

Before America's entry into the war, Czechs
enlisted in the Canadian army. Others
joined the Czechs fighting the Central Powers alongside the Allies after having deserted the Austrian army; the 28th Prague
Regiment for instance went over to the Allies
as a body. In the course of the war, close
to 3,000 American Czechs and Slovaks joined
the Czechoslovak Legions in France, others
the ones in Russia and Italy.

1917 February. After previous vetoes by Cleveland and Taft, Congress passed over Wilson's veto the law making literacy a condition for immigration. The Czechs were little affected by it.

The Czechs felt pressured by the combined influence of the Germans and Irish, who, disliking the British, were inclined to join forces with Britain's enemy. When Chicago's mayor threatened to punch the King of Enggland in the nose, the Germans and Irish cheered, but the Czechs jeered.

February 5. Czech Catholics had been supporting the Alliance as individuals. Upon the prodding of Cleveland's father Oldrich Zlámal, they now as a group joined the work of the Alliance, forming the Národní svaz českých katolíku (National Alliance of Czech Catholics).

February. The Alliance financed the monthly Bohemian Review; after November, 1918 its name was changed to Czechoslovak Review. It was published in Chicago until 1924.

April 6. The United States declared war on Germany on April 6, and on Austria-Hungary on December 7, joining the Allies as an "associate power." The socialists opposed the war, but the Czech socialists favored it for ethnic reasons. A total of 40,000 Czech and Slovak Americans served in the U.S. forces. According to Č.S.P.S. sources, the Alliance members sold the highest proportion of U.S. War Bonds of the ethnic population, with a $38.50 average that was higher than the national one.

April. The Czech Press Bureau in New York, under the leadership of Charles Pergler, succeeded in having senator William S. Kenyon of Iowa and Congressman Adolph J. Sabath of Illinois introduce resolutions in Congress favoring the establishment of a Czechoslovak state.

Olga Štastná, M.D. of Wilber, Nebraska, made a five minute speech on Americanization, which was adopted by the U.S. National Defense Council and used in its campaigns.

1918

January 8. President Wilson proclaimed his Fourteen Points as a blueprint for future peace. They included self-determination for the nations of Austria-Hungary. The last point dealt with the establishment of a League of Nations to guarantee the territorial and political independence of all nations, a concept not too remote from the plan put forward by the Czech king George of Poděbrad in 1464.

February 12. As a summit organization the Československá národní rada (Czechoslovak National Council) was established, combining representatives of the Czech National Alliance, the Slovak League and the Czech Catholic Alliance. Its board, elected on October 17th, 1918, in Cleveland, was headed by American born professor Bohumil Šimek; Albert Mamatey of the Slovak League and father Innocent Kestl of the Catholic group were vice-presidents. Vojta Beneš, brother of Dr. Eduard Beneš, who had lectured extensively about the cause in America for several years, was elected secretary.

May 5. Professor Masaryk received a triumphant welcome by his "brothers and sisters" in Chicago. The Czech press recorded a crowd of 150,000 at the rally where he spoke. His receptions at Cleveland, Boston, Baltimore and Pittsburg were similar.

May 25. Masaryk spoke at Carnegie Hall in New York. Joseph A. Knedlhans designed a flag of the future republic by placing a blue triangular wedge on the red and white Czech flag. Thus the Czechoslovak flag was first flown in America from the mast of the Plaza Hotel, where Masaryk was staying.

May 31. The Pittsburgh Agreement was signed between the Czechs and Slovaks dealing with their future relations within Czechoslovakia.

October 18. The Czechoslovak Declaration of Independence was proclaimed in Washington, D.C. One of the men helping with the draft was Louis D. Brandeis, whose parents came from Prague.

November 11. In the farewell address to his American compatriots, Masaryk declared that

they held an assured place of honor in the
liberation of their ancestral land. This
praise was reflected on the United States
as a whole, traditionally esteemed by the
inhabitants of Czechoslovakia.

Willa Cather's My Antonia, dealing with
Czech pioneer life in Nebraska, was published.

1920 Having accomplished its main mission, the
Czechoslovak National Council turned to cultural affairs. During the years between the
two wars, it supported the exchange of students, scholars and artists; several concert
tours of choirs and opera singers were undertaken. The Council sponsored the publication of a textbook by Bohumil Mikula, Progressive Czech, which went through several
editions.

Between 1917 and 1920 fewer than one thousand Czechs immigrated to the United States.
The lowest figure was 74 in 1918. The auto-
mobile era contributed to the dispersion of
the Czechs within the cities. As the members
of the second generation achieved better
education and intermarried with other nationalities, they blended into the fabric of the
American tableau. In proportion to the growth
of the U.S. population, the number of Czechs
was diminishing. The telltale sign of the
fate of the group was contained in the de-
clining figures of their periodicals, which
shrank to 80, few if any with a circulation
over 30,000.

America counted 622,000 first and second
generation Czechs, 234,000 and 388,000 respectively. Two thirds were living in urban
areas. By now it was taken as a matter of
course if a Czech was elected to the state
or local legislature, or as a mayor or judge.

As a whole the Czech community fared well.
If they had one or two millionaires among
them, they were inconspicuous. The Bulova
watch company and the Waldes company that
made fasteners (later zippers), both on Long
Island, were two businesses that grew considerably during the post-war years. Charles
Stáva of Newark was the first Czech to pur-
chase a seat at the stock exchange. There
were over 90 Czech banks with a capital of

over $ 75 million, five of them in Chicago.
Czech Chicago could support 106 building and
loan associations. A few Czechs were putting
on airs and were quickly dubbed "potato aris-
tocracy" by their own people. The majority
were hard working middle class folk, as content or discontent with their lot as their
neighbors.

1921 May 19. Congress enacted a temporary Emergency Quota Act that for the first time restricted immigration on a quantitative basis.
According to a formula of 3 % of the number
of nationals residing in the U.S. in 1910,
the combined quota for Czechs and Slovaks
was established at 14,282. The high numbers
of immigrants during the three years following the passage of this act can be accounted
for by the backlog of those who intended to
immigrate during the war, but were prevented
from doing so by the hostilities; by the
haste of those who feared that immigration
to America could be drastically limited in
the near future; and by the departure of
those who were not pleased with the new political arrangements in Czechoslovakia.

Violinist Otakar Ševčík, arrived in the United States and became professor at the conservatory at Ithaca, N.Y.

Music has been a common predilection and
profession of Czechs, giving rise to the
saying, "Co Čech to muzikant" - "Every Czech
a musician." The American Federation of
Musicians in Cleveland, for instance, listed
179 Czech names, 12 from the Hrubý family a-
lone, and almost as many Zámečníks.

1923 In Bohemia, N.Y. a pearl button factory was
established.

The Czech word "robot" became part of the
English language. It came from Karel Čapek's
play R.U.R. (Rossum's Universal Robots) that
dealt with robots revolting against their
creators; the play was produced in London
and New York.

1924 May 26. Congress enacted the National Origins Act. The quota formula was changed
from 3% to 2%, and the base year from 1910
to 1890. Under the new law, the Czechoslovak

quota was 3,073, or less than 25% of the
previous one.

1925   The era of the "red-scare" diminished the
ranks of the Czech socialists. Their center was Cleveland. They were active in the
struggle for old age pensions in Ohio, in
the strike of the Amalgamated Clothing Workers and in the co-operative movement. One
of their ablest men was Joseph Martínek,
president of a consumer co-operative; he
founded the Czech co-operative village Tábor
near Cleveland.

Four socialist weeklies were still being
published: Zájmy lidu (Interests of the People, 1898-1930) in Chicago; Spravedlnost
(Justice, 1905-1930), the second one of this
name, also in Chicago; Americké dělnické
listy (American Workingmen's Gazette, 1908-
1953) in Cleveland; and Obrana (Defense,
1910-1938) first in New York, then in Chicago; at a time it was also a daily.

1926   Dr. Aleš Hrdlička of the Smithsonian Institution embarked on the first of his expedi-
tions to Alaska to study the Eskimos and
the Aleuts.

Tomáš Čapek published in Prague Naše Amerika
(Our America) which became very popular.

1929   July 1. The National Origins Act was adjusted once more. The Czechoslovak quota
went from 3,073 to 2,874. For the sake of
comparison: the quota of Great Britain was
65,721 and never exhausted, of the USSR
2,784, and of China 100.

October 24. On Black Thursday, the stock-
market began to crash. Czechs were not
among the large stockholders; but the community was affected by the resulting depres-
sion, loss of employment and by bank failures.
Thousands of Czechs were among the millions
of jobless workers, and many lost their
businesses or their farms through foreclo-
sures. The crisis played havoc with the
small Czech banks and building and savings
associations, half of which went bankrupt.
All this affected the life of the various
clubs and associations, which had their
funds deposited in small banks. Members did

not have the money to pay dues, and a large
number of ethnic activities came to an end,
never to resume again.

1930   The numbers of the Czechs kept diminishing;
        in 1920 there were 234,000 Czechs in the
        country, in 1930 only 201,000.

1932   December 27. At the Č.S.P.A. congress in
        Chicago, four other major fraternal or bene-
        volent federations joined with the Č.S.P.S.
        and created the Československé Spolky v
        Americe (Czechoslovak Society of America),
        or Č.S.A. for short.

        The merging organizations were: Č.S.P.S.,
        founded in 1854, with 208 lodges; the Union
        of Taborites, founded in 1880, with 42 lodges;
        the Czecho-Slavic Fraternal Benefit Union,
        founded in 1884, with 88 lodges; the Czecho-
        Slavic Union, founded in 1892, with 52 lodges;
        and the Independent Order of Forester Men and
        Women, founded in 1899, with 30 lodges. The
        number of lodges of the newly formed Č.S.A.
        was 420, with a membership of 24,613. Over
        the future years, still other federations
        joined the Č.S.A.

1933   February 15. Chicago's mayor Anton Čermák
        stopped the assassin's bullet intended for
        Franklin Delano Roosevelt in Miami. Čermák
        was the first foreign born mayor of Chicago;
        he came from Kladno, a coal mining town near
        Prague and started out as a coalminer. He
        lies buried at the Czech National Cemetery
        in Chicago.

1936   The Texas state legislature erected a momu-
        ment commemorating the oldest Czech settle-
        ment at Hostyn (then called Bluff) in 1856.

1937   The Masaryk Institute was founded in New
        York to foster cultural relations between
        the United States and Czechoslovakia. After
        the war broke out in Europe, much of its
        activity was taken up in war relief work and
        the care of refugees. It located scholarships
        for refugee students and employment for
        scholars.

1938   May 21. Under the growing danger of Nazi
        expansion, Czechoslovakia mobilized. The
        Czech National Alliance was then reactivated

and a Slovak National Alliance was organized.

September 26. During the Munich crisis, with the participation of many sympathisers, including American labor, the Czechs organized a rally at the Chicago Stadium, which was their largest manifestation for democracy since the time that Masaryk had arrived during World War I; 65,000 people attended. Paul H. Douglas was the main speaker.

September 30. As a consequence of the Munich decision, the dismemberment of Czechoslovakia commenced. An estimated 20,000 people fled before Nazi persecution, and several thousand found refuge in America. About 25% were in the professions, with a number of scholars and artists among them.

1939   February. Exiled president Eduard Beneš came to the University of Chicago to deliver a series of lectures; at the same time he re-established contact with his American compatriots.

March 15. The Germans marched into Prague; they established a "Protectorate" over the historic lands of Bohemia and Moravia; Slovakia was set up as an independent country under a puppet president, Monsignor Jozef Tiso.

March 15. The same day in Chicago's Pilsen Park there was a demonstration against the occupation, with Jan Masaryk, son of the former president as main speaker. He was to become the foreign minister of the government in exile.

March 25. A "Stop Hitler" march was organized in New York. Czechoslovaks had sufficient clout to keep their pavillion at the World's Fair open.

July 2. A rally of 25,000 listened to Dr. Beneš in New York.

September 1. The war broke out in Europe.

November 1. The Czecho-American Union, founded in 1910, joined the Č.S.A.

November 17. Czech universities were per-

manently closed by the Nazi occupation; hundreds of students were sent to concentration
camps in Sachsenhausen and Oranienburg, and
several executed. In America, public protests were held against the massacre of the
Czech students.

1940   The Czech National Alliance had 213 chapters
in 14 regions, with over 30,000 members. It
carried the heaviest financial burden in the
Czechoslovak National Council in America.

The Czechoslovak National Council was the
top coordinating body, closely co-operating
with the Czechoslovak government in exile in
London. As during the first World War, it
combined the efforts of the Czech Alliance,
the Czech Catholics and the Slovak National
Alliance. The Slovak separatists were not
part of it, nor were the leftists, who toed
the Soviet line during the time of the Ger-
man-Soviet pact. This time, however, the
task of the Council was harder, for there
were only half as many people to carry it
out; their average age was close to 60.
There were 30% fewer publications as communication channels.

During the war the Council published News
Flashes From Czechoslovakia, a monthly issued in Chicago, with a circulation of 25,000;
it subsidized over a dozen publications in
three languages; it published 20 books in
English, and supplied press releases as well
as lecturers to schools, churches and clubs.
It maintained a broadcasting service from
Boston to occupied Czechoslovakia. It offered aid to refugees and to soldiers who
once again were joining the Allies as legion-
naires.

The Czechoslovak Red Cross was established
in Chicago by Dr. Alice Masaryk, Vlasta Vráz
and Betka Papánek; thousands of women were
involved in its program. The Č.S.A. contributed $ 50,000.

The Bata Shoe Company was established in
Belcamp, Maryland. The Bata family were
shoemakers since the 17th century, and theirs
was one of the largest corporations in Czechoslovakia. Now Bata of Maryland has branches
in 90 countries.

1941   Composer Bohuslav Martinů arrived in America.

December 7. Pearl Harbor was attacked by Japan. The following day the United States entered the war.

1942   June 12. A crowd of 50,000 attended the naming of a township near Joliet, Illinois, Lidice, in commemoration of the Czech village that the nazist occupiers raised to the ground, shooting all men, transporting the women into concentration camps, and sending the small children to Germany for adoption. The main speaker was Wendell Wilkie, "delegated by F.D.R."

With America at war, Czech efforts concentrated on the sale of bonds. Č.S.A. purchased $ 4 million war bonds, receiving as a reward the Minuteman Banner. For its contributions, a B-52 bomber was named "Czechoslovak Society of America." Č.S.A. waived payments of premiums for men in the armed forces, yet paid full death claims for the 103 of its members who lost their lives in the war. It collected a monthly 5 ¢ "freedom tax" from all members toward the liberation of the ancestral country.

1943   November 30. "Miss Liberty" Evelyn Mládková sold $ 1.2 million bonds and was given the privilege of christening the liberty ship <u>Anton J. Cermak</u> in Baltimore.

1944   The American Relief for Czechoslovakia was organized. It later received over $ 4 million from the National War Fund. The Czech Alliance contributed $ 322,000, the Č.S.A. $ 50,000. Kenneth D. Miller directed the relief work.

1945   After the end of the war Vlasta Vráz of Chicago represented the American Relief in Prague. The aid continued until 1949. In addition, post-war aid from American friends and relatives amounted to about $ 10 million.

1946   Gerty and Carl F. Cori, both born in Prague, shared the Nobel Prize for physiology.

1947   Cultural exchange resumed, and the first exchange students arrived in America. At the University of Chicago a Masaryk Club was

founded; similar clubs sprang up at other
colleges, analogous to the Komenský clubs of
the early 1900's.

1948   February 25. In a coup, the communists took
over the government in Czechoslovakia. A
new stream of refugees started arriving in
America, among them a large proportion of students and teachers, journalists and professional people.

In the spring the American Fund for Czechoslovak Refugees was established in New York,
sponsored by Eleanor Roosevelt, Marcia Daven-
port, Drew Pearson, governors Lehman and
Lausche, and others. Financing came from
the Council and from donations. It has been
under the direction of Dr. Jan Papánek ever
since. The Fund helped resettle thousands
of refugees after 1948 and again after 1968.
In the 19 years of its existence, it dis-
bursed over $ 3 million.

June 3. The Czechoslovaks in America presented a memorandum to President Truman demanding
free elections in their ancestral country.
Meanwhile, they signed hundreds of affadavits
for refugees and provided them with jobs.

The Displaced Persons Act was the first of
8 special acts between 1948 and 1960, pro-
viding for the admission of refugees from
communist dominated countries, victims of
natural calamities and orphan children.

Through the Masaryk Institute in New York,
American colleges and universities offered
aid to students and professors. At Harvard
and the Massachusetts Institute of Techno-
logy, there were at times 50 refugee   students, at the University of Chicago 32, each
on scholarships. Mathematician Václav
Hlavatý, who had worked with Albert Einstein,
started teaching at Indiana University.
This group adjusted to America faster than
the earlier immigrants.

Former members of Parliament in Prague who
were refugees in America, organized the
Council of Free Czechoslovakia in Washington,
D.C.

The women formed their own National Council

of Women in Exile, headquartered in Chicago.
Their purpose was to keep alive the spirit
of two women executed by the nazis and the
communists respectively: Františka
Plamínková of the women's movement and Dr.
Milada Horáková, member of Parliament. By
the time the 1968 influx of refugees started
arriving, they were able to help the newcomers.

1952   The McCarran-Walters Act changed the Czecho-
        slovak immigration quota slightly, lowering
        it by 15.

1953   Colonel Frank J. Kobes, graduate of West
        Point, became the Director of Physical Edu-
        cation at that academy; he was brought up
        as a Sokol in Crete, Nebraska.

1954   Č.S.A. in its hundredth year had 213 Czech
        lodges and 110 English speaking lodges, with
        47,146 members in 22 states, most in Illi-
        nois, Ohio and New York. These figures did
        not include the Texan and Western federa-
        tions, with a total of about 80,000 members.

1956   Rear Admiral George J. Dufek during opera-
        tion "Deep Freeze" was the first American
        at the geographic South Pole.

1957   Communist sympathisers were defeated in
        their attempt to take over the Czech free-
        thinkers movement in Chicago.

1957   March 1. The Czechoslovak National Council
        started publishing two monthlies from Chi-
        cago: Věstník (Bulletin) and The American
        Bulletin in English. Both still exist.

1958   June. At the impetus of Dr. Jaroslav Němec,
        200 intellectuals founded the Společnost
        pro vědy a umění (Czechoslovak Society of
        Arts and Sciences in America), or S.V.U.
        The mathematician Václav Hlavatý was its
        first president. While the membership op-
        poses any form of totalitarianism, S.V.U.
        is a non-political, cultural organization
        of scholars, artists and professionals.
        It has maintained a publication program and
        held bi-annual congresses. Since 1959 it
        has published a monthly, Zprávy S.V.U. (News
        of S.V.U.), and since 1964 the literary
        quarterly Proměny (Metamorphoses). Among

the present 1,500 members are (or were) Ru-
dolph Firkusný, Karel Husa, Karel Jirák and
Rafael Kubelík in the field of music, the
writers Ivo Ducháček and Egon Hostovský,
historian Otakar Odložilík, literary critic
René Wellek, actor George Voskovec, and
professors at over a hundred American institutions of higher learning.

1960   March 7. The U.S. Post Office issued in its
            "Champions of Liberty" series a 4 ¢ and an
            8 ¢ stamp honoring Thomas G. Masaryk. Al-
            legedly the Czechoslovak postal service re-
            turned letters with these stamps as unde-
            liverable.

            The Augustine Herrman Historical Society
            placed his bust, made by Norma Švejda, in
            the State House at Baltimore.

1961   The American Jewish community established
            the Society for the History of Czechoslovak
            Jews in New York.

1962   The weekly Americké listy (American Gazette)
            was launched in New York.

1963   The Svaz svobodných československých
            sportovcú (Association of Free Czechoslovak
            Sportsmen) was founded. Among the members
            are former stars like hockey player Pepa
            Malecek, soccer player Jan Havlíček (not to
            be confused with John Havlicek, the basket-
            ball player, whose father was Czech), and
            present stars like skater Aja Zanova (Vrzáňová).
            The club has extended an invitation to ten-
            nis player Martina Navrátilová.

            October 3. The immigration quotas were
            abolished, the law to take effect as of
            July 1, 1968.

1966   April. The exiled archbishop of Prague,
            now cardinal Josef Beran, was honored by
            the Czech community of America from New
            York to Texas.

            October 21. Czech refugee and American ci-
            tizen Vladimír Kazan-Komárek was taken off
            the plane at an unscheduled landing at
            Prague and held for three months in a case
            that attracted international attention. La-
            ter he disappeared mysteriously on a flight

in Canada.

1968 August 20-21. Warsaw Pact troops invaded
Czechoslovakia and put an end to the Dubček
aspirations "to humanize communism." [An
aide at the Nixon campaign headquarters is
reported to have said: "What a break! This
Czech thing is just perfect. It puts the
soft-liners in a hell of a box!"] Hundreds
of Czechs fled to America; most were young
or middle aged, skilled and educated, and
located jobs with relative ease. While in
World War I and II the Czech ethnic group
in America was united for the liberation of
their ancestral lands from a foreign element,
in 1948 and again in 1968 it has been far
from a consensus in evaluating the political
situation. Aside from natural attrition and
the drying up of the immigration flow, this
lack of consensus contributes toward the
fading trend of their ethnic existence.

October 18-20. At the commemoration of the
50th anniversary of Czechoslovak independence,
memorial services were held at the Washington National Cathedral for Woodrow Wilson.
The group called attention to the new op-
pression in their homeland, and manifested
its "faith and dedication to American principles of democracy."

October 28. The day was declared Day of Free
Czechoslovak Culture by a dozen states and
several dozen cities all over the United
States.

1970 Czechs - and the rest of the civilized world -
commemorated the 300th anniversary of Komenský's death.

1972 December 7. Apollo 17 carried Eugene Cernan
of Chicago Czech descent toward a lunar land-
ing. With this third mission, he logged
close to 500 hours in space.

1975 Between June 30, 1946 and June 30, 1975,
27,049 Czechoslovak refugees were admitted
to the United States. The figure for the
last of these years was 118.

December. The Catholic periodicals Katolík
and Národ, published by the Czech Benedictine
Press, folded.

1976   January 1. The weekly <u>Hlas</u> <u>národa</u> (<u>Voice of</u>
            <u>the Nation</u>) was launched, edited by father
            Vojtěch Vít and published in Chicago by the
            Czech-American Heritage Center. The Czech
            Catholic voice was becoming smaller; yet it
            included the archbishops of Indianapolis,
            George Biskup, and of Galveston-Houston,
            John L. Morkovský.

            The American Bicentennial was celebrated in
            Czech centers with speeches, lectures and
            musical performances. The Council in Chi-
            cago honored it with a gala concert. The
            theme of the Washington, D.C. congress of
            S.V.U. in 1976 was the Czech and Slovak con-
            tributions to the United States.

1977   June 19. John Nepomucene Neumann, who im-
            migrated from the small Czech town of Strakonice
            in 1836 to become the bishop of Philadelphia,
            was canonized in Rome, the first male saint
            from the United States.

                                    *

            The body of Czech immigrants arrived at a
            propitious time; that, and their affinity
            with America for hard work, freedom of con-
            science and the simple pleasures of life, re-
            sulted in a combination fortunate for both.
            As the melting pot theory is being challenged
            in favor of pluralism, the Czech immigrants,
            and others, are being absorbed into the na-
            tional fabric.

            It might be true that a quarter of the Cedar
            Rapids population is of Czech descent or that
            452,812 people claimed the Czech mother tongue
            in 1970; that Czech is still taught in a
            handful of schools or that senator Roman
            Hruska or Congressman Charles Vanik of Ohio
            are of Czech origin. The naked facts remain
            that the <u>Denní</u> <u>Hlasatel</u> is the only Czech
            daily left, and that barely 80,000 Czechs
            born abroad live in this country. Ethnic
            enthusiasm will flare for a considerable
            time, as in the case of Boston, where the
            ailing Masaryk Club in April, 1977 co-sponsored
            the opera "Bartered Bride" at Tufts Univer-
            sity, and Czechs from neighboring states
            flocked to it. But in an era when patriotism
            is considered an old fashioned sentimentalism,

the dedication of the younger Czech generations is less inspired than it used to be
in the days of the Rosickýs, Zlámals or
Martíneks. Be it not in vogue theoretically,
in practice the descendants of the Czechs
are melting into their cherished America.

The above chronological mosaic is but the
cover on the Czech immigrants' history.
The book itself has an infinite number of
pages.

DOCUMENTS

In the following documentation about Czech immigrants care has been taken to present a tableau that would illustrate their geographical distribution, urban and rural settlements, their material as well as their spiritual experiences.

It is tragic that of the numerous Czech periodicals published in the United States so few copies survive. A sorrowful example of their fate is the Chicago daily <u>Svornost</u>, published since 1875. When it folded in 1957, its complete archives were destroyed. Partly as a result of this irreplaceable loss to history, Zdeněk Hruban, M.D. and Dr. Václav Laška, both refugees, became instrumental in establishing the Czech and Slovak Immigration Archives at the University of Chicago Library in 1970.

An abundance of Czech periodicals, collections of correspondence and other materials pertaining to overseas Czechs had been preserved at the Institute of Foreign Relations, the Náprstkovo Museum and other depositories in Prague, but repeated inquiries to those sources brought no response. It can be only hoped that papers still in private collections, or those of ethnic lodges, schools, churches, associations and clubs would find their way to the newly established repository at Chicago.

Personal recollections of "old timers" have been compiled by several historically minded Czechs, expanded with the help of their own memories and by copying laboriously pages from newspapers and almanacs, that once used to gather dust in a few attics. Through their labor of love these local historians rendered an invaluable service: they preserved for us a good part of the laughter and tears, hopes and frustrations of the Czech beginnings in America. Their legacy mirrors life a century ago, when Czech horsemen rode over the Rockies in search of gold, or stood poised for the shot that opened the great run for Oklahoma lands. Czech immigration parallels American urbanization, and to an unexpected degree the westward move of the frontier. This, more than official documents, brings to life men and women who helped build America.

It has been a thorny road from Augustine Herrman, sailing for weeks in 1633 to reach the promised land, to the latest arrivals after the fading of the "Dubček Spring" of 1968, who winged their way to their refuge; an equally arduous path led from the laborer hauling boards and falling into icy waters in mid-nineteenth century Chicago, to the professor of philosophy, who arrived in the late 1960's and a few weeks later faced his students in a classroom.

Let the documents and those who lived the history speak for themselves.

LORD OF BOHEMIA MANOR

Augustine Herrman from Mšeno was the
first Czech immigrant known by name,
who settled in America. For drawing
a map of Maryland - that was to be used
for the next two centuries - he received
from Lord Baltimore 20,000 acres of land,
that he named Bohemia Manor. He was also made the first naturalized "denizen"
of any American colony in 1660.

Source: Proceedings, Council of Maryland, 1660.

Caecilius absolute Lord and Proprietary of the Pro-
vinces of Maryland and Avalon Lord Baron of Baltemore
&c. To all Persons to whom these presents shall Come
Greeting in our Lord God Euerlasting. Whereas Augustine
Herman late of Manhatans Marchant haueing of long tyme
used the trade of this our Province hath besought vs to
grant vnto him leaue to transporte himselfe and family
into this our Province here to inhabit, And for our
satisfaction and the benefitt of trade hath drawne a
Mapp of all the Riuers Creekes and Harbours therevnto
belonging Know yee that Wee . . . Doe hereby Declare
him the said Augustine Herman to be a free Denizen of
this our Province of Maryland And Doe further for vs
our heires and Successors straightly Enioyne Constitute
Ordaine and Command that the said Augustine Herman be
in all things held treated reputed and esteemed as One
of the faithfull People of vs our heires and Successors
. . . without the lett molestation Vexation trouble or
Grieuance of vs our heires and Successors and Custome
to the Contrary hereof in any wise notwithstanding.
Given at Saint Maryes Vnder the Great Seale of our said
Province of Maryland the ffowerteenth day of January
in the Nyne and twentieth yeare of our Dominion over
the said Province of Maryland Annoque Domini One thousand Six Hundred and Sixty. Wittnes our Deare brother
Philip Calvert Esquier our Lieutenant of our said Province of Maryland.

EARLY CZECH IMMIGRANTS TELL THEIR STORIES

Source: Rudolf Bubeníček, comp. Dějiny
Čechů v Chicagu, Chicago, 1939.

The information about the first known
Czech in Chicago surfaced from an unexpected source, the periodical České
osady v Americe, published in Hamburg.
In the July 1, 1888 issue there was an
obituary: "One of the oldest, if not
the oldest Czecho-American settler,
Vojtěch Skliba, died recently. He came
to America in the year 1846 and lived
in Chicago a full 42 years." The rest
was detective work by Bubeníček, the
compiler, who for years had been gath-
ering reminiscences of old-timers, or
copying them from unpublished diaries
and from newspapers no longer available.
Had it not been for him, much of the
flavor of the Czech beginnings, the
human side of history, would have been
lost to posterity.

Vojtěch came to Chicago with his mother, when he
was 12 years old. He learned the trade of saddler and
harness-maker and opened a shop on former Michigan
Street, on the north side of the town, between State
and Dearnborn Streets, nearer to State. But he did not
just make saddles and harnesses, he also got into the
carriage trade and in time he employed as many as 15
workmen and drivers. In those days his business was
truly a gold mine, nobody was dreaming of automobiles,
and he became considerably prosperous. He wedded a
Czech girl, Petríková, with whom he had seven children.
The first child, daughter Stela, died in early youth,
the second one was daughter Alberta, then followed in
succession sons Josef, Albert, Robert, Emil and Frank.
All sons worked with the father. . . . Vojtěch Skliba
passed away on April 24, 1888, when he was only 54 years
old. His wife preceded him in death by a few years.
Skliba was brought up in the Catholic religion; but he
visited often with his relatives, the Kučeras (who
lived on Chicago Avenue, next to Noble Street), and the
violent debates about the church and about priests in
this strongly Catholic family made him lose his faith
completely. In the big fire of 1871 the Skliba family

lost all their property. . . .   Škliba and his wife were
burried in Graceland Cemetery in Chicago. . . .
     If Vojtĕch Škliba was the first Czech immigrant who
settled in Chicago, then we must consider his mother,
whose Christian name we could not ascertain, the first
Czech woman in Chicago.

              Jan Novák came to America in 1852,
              and while he often sighed after his
              old homeland, he was satisfied with
              his new life. He described why and
              how they came to settle in Wisconsin.

     In 1851 I happened to see a letter of a certain
Czech from America, who settled in St. Louis, in which
he drew a picture of American life and freedom; thus I
got the idea, that I shall with my family also look for
a new and free home beyond the ocean.   I petitioned for
a permit; although I made their life uncomfortable,
still for fourteen weeks they put all kinds of hurdles
in my way, and I was forced to undertake six trips to
the county seat six hours away, and only after I declared that I would have to make inquiries at the re-
gional government in Budĕjovice, why it was that I could
not get the permit, only then was I told to return home,
and if my passport would still not be at the office of
the local authorities, then I shall obtain it in a short
while.   Sure enough the third day my wife was called to
the official, and because they had known that they would
get nowhere with me, they wanted at least to talk my
wife into opposing my idea; but they were mistaken in
her. . . .
     So many neighbors gathered, that the highway lead-
ing around our house was full of people, who came for
the last time to shake my hand, and with tears in my
eyes I said for ever good bye to them.   I was accompanied three hours of the way to the river Kamejka by at
least forty faithful neighbors, and from there I took
off by ship to Prague with my wife Anna and our one
year old daughter.   I stayed three days in Prague in order to look over for the last time the capital of Čechia
[sic] and then took off by train to Hamburg. . . .
     We boarded a sailship, that brought us in 26 days
to New York; the voyage was stormy, and the treatment
we received was rough. . . .   The trip by train from
New York to Chicago took six days.   When we arrived, I
left my wife and baby at the station and went to look
for some place to stay.   When I returned I saw an old
Czech standing next to my wife; he offered to take us
to a place to stay, which was exactly what happened.
In half an hour we rented two rooms, for which we paid
3 dollars a month; the same day we got a few things for

the household that were absolutely necessary, and after
resting after the long and tiresome trip, I started looking for work, which I found. Many railroads were being
built, so I got a job unloading rails from a ship, which
lasted 14 days. The pay was one dollar and 25 cents for
ten hours of work. Here I made the acquaintance of some
Germans, who had lived there for some time, and they always found a job for me, but at times dangerous jobs.

Once, when we had to load meat, because there were
no steam tugboats yet, we had to pull the ship for one
mile up the river to the stockyards, my foot slipped,
and I fell into the river, that already had half an inch
of ice. I knew how to swim well and I got to the shore,
where I grabbed a board, that was not fastened, and fell
into the river again. Never mind, I tried to climb out
again and made it, but it was quite an excellent bath.
I ran home, got into dry clothes and went back to work.
The next day we were unloading stone from the ship, and
the wheel and I fell into the water, and I had to re-
trieve [the wheelbarrow] also. My Irish fellow worker
thought it funny, but he ended up the same way, for not
an hour had passed, and the Irishman and his wheel also
fell into the water; and because he did not know how to
swim, there was nothing I could do but jump back into
the water and fish him out.

The winter was nearing, and jobs in the city were
not to be had. I was then forced to go to the woods six
miles away and fell trees, which was of course hard work
and little pay. They paid 60 cents per cart, and that
lasted only six weeks, because too many people came for
this job. I could write more about Chicago, but I think
this is enough. I must mention that I met there only
six Czech families, and one day, when I went to the
store of a Pole, I found there a few Czech families, who
were readying to move to Wisconsin. Among them was also
one man from the same region as I, whose wife was unable
to undertake a trip, and he was forced to remain over
the winter in Chicago. I got acquainted with this man,
and when in the spring there were no jobs, we agreed
that we shall take a look at Wisconsin also. At the beginning of March 1853 we started off on foot to Racine,
because there was no railroad yet from Chicago to the
north. It took us two and a half days. When we arrived
in town, we found no Czechs, but we found out that the
Czechs who had left Chicago, settled about six miles
north of Racine. Indeed, we found them there. We
looked over the whole region around Racine, which was
then hardly populated, and right away I purchased myself
ten acres. . . .

> In March of 1853 František Přibramský
> arrived in Chicago; he was a 23 years
> old tailor from Horaždovice with a

> young bride. His father disinherited
> him for wanting to marry her.

The beginnings in Chicago were very difficult. We
rented a small room, in which stood a bed that somebody
had given us, one chair, a table for sewing, and that
was it. The featherbed we left in New York. The neighbor in the next room had a stove and he let some of the
heat come into our room, so we could at least work. On
the bed we put some straw and covered ourselves with a
coat and a skirt. At night we gathered some wood for
the neighbor to show our appreciation for his heat. Later we received a table, two irons and a bench, so I
could go start looking for work. Then we bought a
stove, bed, chair, and so during the first year we
could save 140 dollars in gold. It was now that we celebrated our wedding with a feast, the Isrealite Kohn
arranged it, he brought a judge, prepared a good dinner,
and suddenly we felt cheerful.

> Josef Kolář was a weaver from Kest-
> řany near Písek, who was also a good
> musician; later he became an innkeep-
> er. He arrived in Chicago in 1853.

Josef Kolář worked for a while in a brazier's shop,
but he mainly supported himself with music. He blew a
bassoon, a clarinet, but no doubt could play other instruments also. The moment a few Czech amateur musicians
arrived in Chicago, he founded with them a "band," the
first Czech orchestra. This one had six members and
used to play in Slavík's tavern. . . . Of course they
played only evenings, for during the day nobody had time
to listen, and the musicians went to work or to gather
wood. Once they got used to playing together well,
they left their jobs and went to make music in the country. First stop was Desplaines, then Elgin, Algonquin
and Wheeling. Hardly were they back in Chicago, they
were engaged for a wedding in Waukegan. Off they went,
with their caps ornamented with ribbons. That was the
only emblem of the band, of which the director and business manager was Kolář and the members were J. Baumeis-
ter, F. Chadima, T. Petraš, J. Tomek and J. Velík.

> Josef Fišer was a 26 year old baker,
> when he came to New York in 1852. He
> lived under the name Rybář and worked
> in the infamous Brooklyn brick factory.
> There were other Czechs there, some un-
> der assumed names still fearing the
> Austrian authorities, whose military
> service they evaded by coming to Ameri-
> ca. Fišer decided that this was not

the life for him; he went West to
seek fame and fortune in Chicago.
He was a wanderer at heart, who
pulled up stakes easily. Yet he
was the first Czech grocer and
first Czech baker in Chicago; he
also had the distinction of being
the first divorced Czech in Chicago. But he wrote his name in the
Czech annals of Chicago by keeping
an immigrants' house from 1864 on;
it was a combination tavern, lodging-
house and restaurant under one roof,
where hundreds of Czech immigrants
found their first shelter and advice. What follows are his pere-
grinations starting in Chicago in
1854.

The very first day he got a job in a lumber warehouse; for one hour of very hard work he got 50 cents
and if he could stand it for a whole day, he could make
five dollars. That was an unheard of income for a
Czech, used to poor wages in New York. Therefore he
wrote to his countrymen, and several came out after him
to Chicago. At first he took any job that came his way.
He moved boards in the warehouse, then was a painter,
then again a common laborer, until he landed a job in
his trade, in a bakery. He delivered the bread all o-
ver town and thus met just about all Czechs, and could
help many, so they later remembered him gratefully. He
spoke German and he could translate at least in that
language for those Czechs who did not know even German;
for this many sought him out. He later started a grocery on the north side of town, and in two years he o-
pened a bakery with František Řeháček of Roudnice.
When his partner did not want to get up early and deliver the pastry, Fišer managed to buy him out.
He married a certain Mrs. Havelková, with whom he
had lots of trouble for she was a flirt. When he could
no longer stand it, he left Chicago first for Wisconsin,
then for St. Louis and New Orleans, and finally settled
in Indianola in Texas, where in Paderborn at the shore
of the Gulf of Mexico he brewed beer in a washing tub
and he also baked bread. In eight months he gathered
a little bundle. Yellow fever broke out there, his
wife kept writing begging him to return, so he decided
to do so. He returned to Chicago in 1858, but he was
weak and sick. His relation with his wife did not get
better, so he had to get a divorce and give her half of
what he had. He married a young Irish girl at the
church of Saint Peter on Polk Street, at night and by

candle light, which made the bride so angry that she never went to a church again. They started all over again.
She was a domestic, he worked, and usually they saw each
other only Saturdays and Sundays. They saved 200 dollars, when fifteen months after the wedding, the young
wife died in childbirth. Fišer left Chicago to see his
countryman Dvořáček in Memphis, but at the beginning of
the Civil War he returned to Chicago, where he got a job
as foreman in a bakery. In 1863 he married for the
third time the widow Vondráčková, née Severinová, who
came to Chicago in 1858. This marriage was happy and
resulted in thirteen babies.

> The casual manner in which some im-
> migrants decided their fate and that
> of their descendants is at times a-
> mazing. Listen to František Stejskal,
> who reached New York on August 19, 1854
> as a boy of twelve. He and his parents
> left their native village near Prague
> "to find happiness and a better existence."

After a long ride, changing trains several times,
we came to the city of Cleveland, where we stayed about
a week, then left for Chicago. In Chicago my father met
a certain fellow-countryman, who had a brother in the
region of Manitowoc in the state of Wisconsin, where he
bought a piece of virgin forest. He recommended that
we should go there too and buy a piece of that forest.
Father brought 600 dollars in gold with him, in those
days a considerable capital, so he had money to pay for
it. I discouraged father from journeying into those
wild forests, I begged him on my knees to stay in Chicago, where I, my two brothers and sister could have a better chance for a school education than in that Wisconsin
desert. But to no avail were my supplications. I was
too young, and my opinion and my begging were not taken
into account; later when father found himself in the
vast woods and had to fight hard, he was sorry he did
not listen to me. Well, father did buy that piece of
the forest in Kossuth Town, about fourteen miles from
Manitowoc, where aside from a few immigrants our neighbors were Indians of the Oneida tribe. What a horrible
struggle for existence, what misery, this is hard to
picture. To create meadows from virgin forests!

> Chicago in the eighteen-fifties was
> becoming a city, with about 70,000
> inhabitants. Still, it had the fea-
> tures of a large village. Václav
> Lhotka remembered:

To meet fellow-countrymen, we went to the church of
St. Peter and Paul on Polk Street and kept looking into
the prayer books to see who was a Czech. Thus we shook
hands and made our acquaintances. On Sundays we liked
to go to the Czech tavern for a little music; the musicians were Jirásek, Kubíček and František Chadima.
There were no streets, no sidewalks, mud to your knees.
My wife carried her shoes in her hands, she went barefoot and put on her shoes only in front of the tavern.

> Jan Slavík from Brno opened the first
> "Czech Tavern" in Chicago in 1855 on
> Clark Street. The hall in this tavern
> was the first gathering place for the
> Czech pioneers. Antonín Pregler re-
> called the tavern with nostalgia.

At his place, at Slavík's, gathered those pathfin-
ders of Czech Chicago, with entertainment like in the
old country, with music of then young musicians, Velík,
Jirásek, Kolár, Vilím and others. And when the hall was
resounding with the old Czech songs like "With what trouble did my little mother bring me up" or "My dear little
Mary, watch it," many an eye of the good old settlers
became filled with tears, and in their memories they all
flew back to the dear old country beyond the ocean, into the native villages and towns. Often it was morning,
when the little sun glittered over the waves of blue
Lake Michigan, that the exhilarated countrymen left the
tavern to return to their poor but welcoming abodes.

> August Geringer was a teacher and a
> bookbinder, born on August 2, 1842
> in Březnice near Písek. He and his
> wife together with several in-laws
> immigrated to America in the summer
> of 1869. Geringer eventually became
> the founder of the oldest Czech daily
> outside Bohemia, the Svornost in Chi-
> cago. In his autobiography, written
> when he was 80 years old, he described
> their trip.

In those days ship travel was not so simple. Every
immigrant had to carry his own tin dishes and carry them
all along during the trip. Our crossing on a steamship

took seventeen days and it was pretty stormy. I was sorry I made the decision to come, but it was too late.
The food on the ship was miserable. We got mostly herring. You had to go with your mess kit to the kitchen,
then eat in some corner, because on the lower decks
there were no tables where immigrants could sit down together and eat comfortably. . . . From New York we left
on the afternoon immigrant train. We had to provide ourselves with some bread, cold cuts and fruit, for on such
trains there was no dining car. We rode until midnight,
then the train stopped, because in those days no trains
could run on Sunday. We were left to fend for ourselves
in the woods the whole Sunday. . . . To have something
to eat, we had to look for a farm; we were lucky and got
some milk.

The trip from New York to Chicago took five full
days, because there were frequent stops, we had to wait
for the regular trains to pass us. In the woods of Ohio
we were attacked. The robbers were shooting into the
carriages, and we had to hide under the seats to avoid
the bullets. This was our welcome to America.

BEGINNINGS IN CHICAGO AND NEW YORK

Source: John Habenicht, Dějiny Čechův
v Americe, St. Louis, 1910; translation
in Francis Dvornik, Czech Contributions
to the Growth of the United States, Chicago, 1962.

Wenceslas Lhota came to Chicago from Bohemia via
Quebec in Canada. The journey in a sailing boat lasted
three months. He arrived in Chicago in absolute poverty,
without a cent, with his wife and eight children. He
constructed a hut from railroad ties, without any windows. He covered the roof with dirt and put an old oven
in his hut, of course, without a chimney. The only fur-
niture was the luggage with his family's clothing which
he brought from home. On New Year's Day 1855 his hut
was destroyed by fire and he was left in the middle of
the winter without any shelter. Fortunately, there was
some work for him on the construction of the railway to
Milwaukee. Then he worked in a tile-kiln and when he
had lost even this job, he wandered through the streets
of Chicago with a saw and an ax, offering his services
for cutting firewood. His son became a prosperous frame
manufacturer.

The early Czech settlers in New York had a particularly hard life. One of them, Frank Brodsky, [ropemaker,
turned steamship agent, arrived 1851], looked in vain
for a long time for a job. He was reduced to such want
that he could not even buy a second-hand pair of shoes.
Ashamed to have to walk barefoot, he blackened his feet
every morning with shoeblack in order to give the impression that he had shoes on and continued his search on
New York streets. At last he found a job on a whale
boat. He made a new start with a few dollars he saved.
Then returning to New York he eventually became a weal-
thy man. Many other early settlers in the cities had
similar experiences.

IN STEERAGE TO THE NEW WORLD

Source: Francis Dvornik, <u>Czech Con-</u>
<u>tributions</u> <u>to</u> <u>the</u> <u>Growth</u> <u>of</u> <u>the</u> <u>Uni-</u>
<u>ted States</u>, Chicago, 1962.

In the eighteen fifties and sixties there were only
a few steamboats plying between Hamburg or Bremen, the
nearest ports to Bohemia, and New York. The price for
this kind of transportation was too high for many immigrants and they had to choose to travel the long and
tiresome journey in sailboats. Sometimes such a voyage
took eight to twelve weeks, owing to storms. One can
imagine the hardships of the unhappy voyage.

The worst trial of this kind was probably experi-
enced by some immigrant families from North East Bohemia
who had decided to settle in Texas in 1852. They had
the misfortune of falling into the hands of an unscrupu-
lous agent in Hamburg who persuaded them to go first to
Liverpool, from where they started their journey to Galveston on the boat "Victoria." The boat was overcrowded
with Irish immigrants. The immigrants were given their
food raw, often spoiled, and every family had to do its
own cooking. Almost all of them got sick and half of
the immigrants died during the voyage which lasted seventeen weeks.

Other Czech immigrants had similar experiences. Josef Safran describes their suffering in the <u>Collection</u>
of the Kansas State Historical Society. He was born in
Central Bohemia. His father, a shoemaker, decided to
immigrate to America in 1856. They started their journey from Bremen to New York on a small sailing vessel
crowded with 250 people in frightful living conditions.
"The food served to the immigrants was so coarse and un-
palatable that young children could not digest it and
cried with hunger. In addition, the drinking water doled
out was barely sufficient to keep down the thirst of the
people. There was none whatever for washing except sal-
ty sea water which was entirely unfit for that purpose.
Looking back now it would seem unendurable, but we and
the others stood it for seven long weeks until we reached
New York."

The journey from New York to Buffalo and then to Detroit and Milwaukee was also tiresome. Safran complained
most about the train journey to Buffalo: "The management
of the New York Central labored under the impression that
immigrants, negroes and cattle were in the same class,
for we rode in common box cars, furnished with rude plank
benches without any backs and a mere excuse for toilet
necessities."

FARMING IN WISCONSIN

The first farming communities of the
Czechs sprung up in Wisconsin in the
1850's and 1860's. The climate was
similar to that of their homeland;
the soil was adaptable to crops familiar to them: rye, wheat, corn, oats,
vegetables. Racine was referred to as
the Czech Bethlehem. Several settlements were in the counties of Manitowoc, Kewaunee, Oconto, LaCrosse, Adams
and Marathon. The war mentioned in
the following article is the Civil War.

Source: Nan Mashek, "Bohemian Farmers
in Wisconsin," Charities, December 3, 1904.

      The early settler bought from forty to sixty acres
of land, making only a small cash payment, and giving a
mortgage for the rest. The price ranged from five to
ten dollars an acre. With the help of his neighbors,
who blazed trails as they came lest they should not be
able to find the way back, he built a log cabin and
felled a few trees to give space for a vegetable patch.
Then came the serious work of clearing the land, and at
the same time earning enough outside money to live and
pay part of the debt. This was accomplished in various
ways. Sometimes the head of the family and the eldest
son worked part of the year in the nearest sawmill or
in the logging camps of northern Michigan. Sometimes
they went to the large farms to the south of Michigan
to help during the harvest. Very often they made hand-
shaved pine shingles of the trees on their land, and exchanged them at the nearest market for what they most
needed.
      These were, indeed, hard years for our pioneers,
but better times came after 1861. The war broke out
and the forest products of which they had such an abundance, increased in price. Tan-bark, cedar posts for
fencing, cord-wood, railroad ties--all found a market
so good that the village shippers bought them as fast
as they could be made and brought to the shipping piers.
Many of these merchant lumbermen advanced money to the
farmers with which to buy oxen and sleighs. They also
took timber products in exchange for flour, cloth and
other necessities, and in other ways the struggle for
existence became less severe, the clearing of the lands
went on more rapidly, and the farmers were able to meet
more easily their living expenses and debts, notwith-

standing war prices on food products and clothes, which put flour at $ 12 a barrel, coffee at 60 cents a pound and ordinary sheeting at 85 cents.

But the war, even with its attendant prosperity, was not an unmixed blessing. Enthusiasm and patriotism, everywhere rife, was further encouraged among the Bohemians by their newspaper The Slavie, then published in Racine, Wis. Many entered the volunteer army, and when later a draft was ordered, large numbers of farms were left without men. There remained usually a large family with only a mother, and perhaps a fourteen-year-old son, to carry on the work of the place, an outlook calculated to overwhelm the most courageous of women. Yet our Bohemian wives were not disheartened and it is remarkable that in all that war-time not one mortgage was foreclosed in Kewaunee county, and not one of these brave women forfeited the homestead that was given into her care.

A PIANO TEACHER ON THE FRONTIER

The first Czech known by name who crossed the continent was the musician Jozef Francl, who left us his diary. On April 18, 1854, at the age of 30, he started out from Watertown, Wisconsin, with four companions, to find gold in California. Later they joined a wagon train. He described buffalo hunts, the beginning of the Sioux war (caused by a lame cow of the Mormon emigrants on August 17, 1854). He found no gold; richer for the experience, he was back in Wisconsin by 1857; became a piano teacher and court clerk of Manitowoc county. By 1870 he established a store in Crete, Nebraska, outfitting emigrants. He died under mysterious circumstances on his trip to California in 1875 and was buried at Fort Klamath.

The poem preceding his diary was written in honor of Nebraskan Czech pioneers by Bartoš Bittner and translated by Libbie B. Scholten.

Source: Rose Rosicky, A History of Czechs (Bohemians) in Nebraska, Omaha, 1929.

With empty hands you came to wilderness uncharted--
Lo, gaze upon it now. O pioneers brave-hearted.
From Father of Waters west to Rocky Mountains' base,
Prosperity's sweet streams those prairies grace.

You triumphed over hardships, weary and heart-
        breaking,
None censures you today for joyful pride you are
        taking,
In your fair handiwork, which far and wide you view,
Instead, success we wish--success to you.

Provisions consisted of 250 pounds hardtack, 150 pounds ham, 50 pounds butter, 50 pounds sugar, 30 pounds coffee, 10 quarts vinegar, 20 pounds beans, 10 pounds peas, spices, axes, chains, rope, augers, saws, 20 pounds gunpowder, 40 pounds lead and shot,--and it was all too scanty for so long a trip. . . .
A trap of willow twigs cought several hundred pounds of fish in a short time. . . . In the Rock River [there were] so many fish of various kinds that one lay

next to the other as far as eye could see. Old inhabitants told me that eight or ten years before that, when
they crossed the river in a wagon, the fish flew about
on all the sides, where the wheels struck them, like so
many shavings. . . .

I would like to describe the effect of a prairie
fire at night, when it is cloudy or the night dark, but
I cannot, words fail me to depict what I feel. It is a
novel, magnificent, immense picture, which deserves the
very ablest description, if I only could do it. A fiery
band, reaching farther than the eye can see, a great
quantity of smoke, and a terrifying glare, all the while
silence reigns, for those who look on do not venture to
speak. It is something incomparably beautiful. . . .

We saw quantities of elk horns, some were 7 feet
long and weighed about 30 pounds. We saw a drove of over
173 elk. They are about as large as a cow, of more slen-
der body, of lighter color than deer, and keep only to
the high prairies. We saw deer at streams. It may be
understood that we did not suffer hunger, for we shot
all the small game we could use. There is one kind of
snipe, about as large as a medium-sized chicken, with
bill about four inches long, that is easy to kill. They
sell for three dollars in the large eastern markets. We
roasted several and at last grew weary of them. The valley here is beautiful. How the water in the great river
glistens and what a strange, crooked course the strong
current makes for itself. How green are the grasses in
this rich valley and what a fertile soil here awaits the
hands of those who will cultivate it. . . .

The trappers appear to me like lunatics. At least
they could never walk the streets of a European town in
their attire. From the remnants hanging in tatters on
their bodies, it is difficult to say whether their clothing is cotton, linen or woolen. Wherever you look,
you can see the owner's dark hide, the rest is covered
with skins of wild animals. The trapper's face has not
seen water during the many hundred miles of his travels.
His hat is made of rough, raw buffalo skin, adorned by
a fox or wolf tail. Some have attached in front the
horns of deer or antelope. When the trapper's trousers
give out, he takes a small buffalo hide, cuts it through
the mouth, dries it by fire and smoke, and behold a pair
of trousers, which he simply pulls on, the skins of the
extremities serving for suspenders. However, his boots
make up for the rest, for they are quite handsome, embroidered by Indian women with beads and ornamented by
a long fine leather fringe. They are very comfortable.
These trappers are an uneducated, Godless sort of people,
and most of them are Frenchmen from Canada. There is an
abundance of game, but these trappers gamble away not only their money but even the last piece of decent clothing,
if they happen to have it, and then go back to hunt again.

The Omaha Indians are of fine, tall bodies. They
paint their faces red and yellow. They smear mud on
their hair, to make it stiff and upright. From the nape
of the neck to the forehead it stands out like a roos-
ter's tail, the rest is clipped close. Their chief has
a different style of head dress. Here the Indians begin
to go about naked, except for a small apron. Some wear
buffalo robes, with designs painted on them, sometimes
embroidered with beads. Their moccasins are of elk or
deer skin. Occasionally an Indian gets or trades for a
pair of trousers, but he does not know that the seat is
to be worn too. He cuts it out entirely and about all
that is left are strings hanging from his sides. Each
Indian carried a board about six inches wide and two
feet long, pointed at the lower end. In the center is
fastened a piece of glass from a mirror and the owner ad-
mires himself therein, adjusting his hair and complexion.
    They would not let us enter their village all to-
gether, for they feared us. So we divided into three
parts, laid aside our weapons and half the Indians accompanied us as guard. We did not see any women. Their
village consists of twenty to thirty huts, made thus:
Eight or ten long poles are arranged in a rounded pyra-
mid, tied firmly at the top, and covered with tanned buffalo hides. The interior contains nothing but animal
skins, which serve for a bed. . . .
    We saw a magnificent sight. If anyone had told me
before I had seen buffaloes that so many are in existence
I would not have believed it. On the other side of the
river, to the left, was a great open space of prairie
covered with buffaloes. As far as eye could reach, nothing but buffaloes. On the horizon great clouds of
dust rose upward, where they were stamping around.
These all belong to the Indian, they are his wealth.
The calves are kept inside the drove, one can see how
the old animals crowd together to protect them. This
so-called buffalo range is about 130 miles in area. . . .
    On the 17th of August, 1854, a party of Mormon emi-
grants on their way to the Great Salt Lake reached a
great camp of thousands of Indians of the Brule, Oglala
and Minneconjou bands, the whole Sioux nation on the
plains, about eight miles east of Fort Laramie, Wyoming.
They were gathered there to receive the goods which the
United States had promised to pay them for the road
through their land. Behind the Mormon wagons lagged a
lame cow driven by a man. When near the Brule Sioux
camp something scared her and she ran into the camp. A
young Minneconjou, Shooters-In-The-Mist, killed her and
his friends helped to eat her. The next day the Mormons
complained to Lieutenant Grattan, commander of Fort Laramie, a young man only twenty-one years old, who had had
no experience with Indians. On the morning of August
19th he set out with twenty-nine men and two cannon and

conferred with the great chief The Bear, who said he
would try to get the young Indian to give himself up.
Grattan said if he would not he would fire and The Bear,
pointing to the thousands of Indian men, women and children, said: "These are all my people. Young man, you
must be crazy." A moment later two cannon and a volley
of muskets were fired at the Sioux camp. The Bear was
killed. A storm of Sioux bullets and arrows cut down
Lieutenant Grattan and his men before they had time to
reload their guns. The Sioux camp went wild and scattered over Nebraska, Wyoming and Dakota, urging Indians
everywhere to kill the white men and drive them from the
country. Thus the Sioux war began. The concensus of
opinion has always been that Lieut. Grattan acted fool-
ishly in this matter.

PETITION FOR A SCHOOL AND A LIBRARY

Yearning for "mental improvement," Czechs
in Racine, Wisconsin, petitioned for a
school and a library on March 3, 1861.

Source: Charles Jonas Papers, State Historical Society of Wisconsin, Madison.

We the undersigned Citizens of the County of Racine in the State of Wisconsin do hereby form ourselves into a Corporation for the purpose of Mental improvement and the promotion of Education and for the purpose of Enlarging, regulating and using ~~that~~ a library for that purpose under and by virtue of the General Statutes of the State of Wisconsin Entitle of Libraries & Lyceums. under the name and Style of The "Slavanska Lipa" Lyceum And Library of the City of Racine Dated Racine March 3ᵈ 1861

Chas. Jonas
M. Mathias Zika
Joseph Novacny
Fr. ...
V. Bobek
A. Kroupa
...
F. ...
J. ...
John Riegle son
Andrew ...
F. W. Drahos
Joseph Welfl
John L. Peters
Frank ...

CZECHS AND INDIANS

As all pioneers on newly settled lands,
the Czechs faced danger from the Indians.
During the Civil War, with army protection being almost non-existent, Indian
raids were frequent. Jan Kašpar of
Hutchison, Minnesota, tells us what it
was like to live in constant fear.

Source: <u>Amerikán</u>, Chicago, 1891

The years 1862 - 1863 will forever live in our memories. Those were the years that the Indians went on
the warpath, murdering white people everywhere and putting to the torch their homes and farms. Half of the
small town of Hutchison was laid to ashes, and many people were murdered in a most brutal manner. There were
fourteen Czech families living there. We all got together on one farm; we enclosed the yard by felling
large trees and building a fortification. The cattle
were driven between this palisade and the farmhouse. We
also deposited all our movable property there. All men
carried arms, even the youngsters handled guns in the
defense of our little fortress. The United States army
could not rush to our defense, they were stationed too
far from our settlement. . . .
    Our fields were not too far from our homes, but we
were scared to venture out because of the Indian danger.
So we farmed only those fields and meadows which were
closest to our houses, and even while we worked, our
loaded guns were right next to us. Towards the end of
1863, the glad tidings reached us that a large contingent
of the army was on its way to our settlement. We heard
this with great relief.

WHAT IS SOKOL?

The Sokol organization was founded
in Prague in 1862. In the United
States the "Sokol Society" was first
founded on February 14, 1865 in St.
Louis. Chicago had its Sokol in
1866, New York in 1867, and soon
there was a Sokol in most Czech settlements in America.

Source: Jarka Jelinek and Jaroslav
Zmrhal, Sokol Educational and Physical Culture Association, Chicago, 1944.

Sokol is a world-wide organization, which trains
both the youth and the adults so that they may become
physically, morally, and mentally fit. The training is
carried on in the patriotic and brotherly spirit.

Everyone belonging to the Sokol must be an honorable
man or woman, so that, as good citizens of the United
States, they may be devoted to their country and be doing their best for its welfare. Religious and party dif-
ferences play no part and have no effect on the membership.

The basis of the Sokol Idea is proper physical development and moral, patriotic, democratic and forward
looking education.

All members willingly submit to the discipline and
the rules of the Sokol organization to which they belong.
They take part in the physical exercises as much as their
age, health, and employment will permit, as well as in
all the educational projects, entertainments, excursions,
meetings and Slets. They always work for the welfare of
their country, and endeavor to lead an exemplary life -
as brothers and sisters.

"Sokol" is an original name for the organization; it
is not translated into other languages. In English it
means "Falcon," a bird known for its courage, endurance,
lightning speed, sharp eyesight and its love of the blue
heights of heavens. Thus it symbolizes the ideals of
the organization: fitness, power and high aims.

Members of the Sokol call each other "brother" -
"sister" and use the familiar "thou." The Sokol greeting is "Nazdar!" meaning "On to success!" The symbol is
a flying falcon.

LINCOLN'S ASSASSINATION

The sailing ship that brought fifteen
year old Wenzl Holý to America took
43 weeks to cross the ocean, and all
passengers suffered hunger. His com-
panion Josef Ženíšek, a tailor from
Pilsen, wanted to get rich quickly
and headed for the silver mines of
Colorado. Holý settled in St. Louis,
eventually became a buyer for a grocery. He married the sister-in-law
of general John McNeill. The marriage
was a happy one but childless. Holý
sent for his nephew from the old
country, Eduard Holý. Following is
Eduard's story.

Source: Rudolf Bubeníček, comp. Dějiny
Čechů v Chicagu, Chicago, 1939.

I shall never forget the 14th of April, 1865.
I was in the Ford Theatre with my uncle and aunt.
They played "Our American Cousin." The moment word got
'round that the president and his lady would attend the
performance, uncle got tickets and in the evening we
went. This theatre was on Seventh Street; it was sold
out. When the president appeared, he was enthusiasti-
cally applauded by the public; most people stood up.
This was just after the splendid victory of general
Grant over the southern general Lee; everybody acknowledged that President Lincoln had the greatest merit in
bringing the war to a victorious end so soon and in sav-
ing the union. Lincoln had been just recently re-elected
and started his second term. The president took a bow
with a serious, fatherly smile on his face, then sat
down and followed the play with great attention. Towards the end of the performance, suddenly there was a
sound of a shot, and in a moment there was general confusion. One could see somebody who jumped from the ban-
ister of the president's box to the stage, fell, but got
up immediately and waved some kind of a dagger over his
head and shouted "The South is avenged," and disappeared
behind the scenery. Right thereafter the news spread in
the theatre that the president was shot. People were
leaving the theatre in sorrow and in confusion, but nobody would or could believe it, when early next morning
the news went the rounds that president Lincoln was dead.
He became the victim of a treacherous assassin, the actor
John Wilkes Booth, who showed his fanatical love for the

defeated slaveholding South and his terrible hatred toward the North by annihilating the life of the greatest
man in the history of our nation. . . . I still remember that the day after President Lincoln died, and for
many more days, people walked around Washington, as if
somebody from their own family had died. Work stopped,
people walked along the streets with heads hanging, they
discoursed quietly, as in the house of a dying person;
it was not rare to see even men, who would suddenly stop
in their tracks, cover their eyes and start crying. Such
was the grief for President Lincoln.

Before I left Washington on November 10, I saw the
execution of Harry Wirtz, a Swiss by birth, who had been
condemned to death because as a commandant of the Andersonville military prison he had tortured in unheard of
ways the captive northern soldiers. Some he kicked to
death, others he had torn to pieces by his enormous dogs.
Among the soldiers who suffered under his tyranny was also our countryman Frank Kouba, the father of Mrs. Fiala,
the wife of Mr. Cyril Fiala in Chicago. If the soldiers
complained that they were dying of hunger, or that their
hands and feet were frozen, Wirtz sicked his two enormous dogs on them; against those even a healthy strong
man would have been powerless. The dog would hurl itself against such a weakened, fatigued prisoner, who often could hardly stand on his feet, grab him with its
incisors by the throat, and in a few minutes of desper-
ate struggle the soldier would let out his soul. And
the beast in human form, Wirtz, would laugh. . . . He
was brought to trial; former prisoners who had seen him
shooting sick prisoners, if he did not prepare some
other form of death for them, bore witness against him.
Wirtz was condemned not to a death of honor by powder
and lead, but to death by hanging. Wirtz's wife, who
was from Kentucky and a member of the organization Ku-
Klux [sic], and his lawyer Shade did all in their power
to receive a pardon from President Johnson for Wirtz,
stating that he only carried out the orders of his com-
manders; but in vain. . . . There was a tremendous
shouting that went up from the northern soldiers--it
still sounds in my ears--when in the Capitol yard the
trapdoor under the gallows opened, and the rope tight-
ened around that throat that in its very last breath was
cursing the United States and was calling the American
eagle a carrion-devouring vulture. . . . I witnessed
this execution with my uncle and shall never forget it.
A few years later, when I was in Chicago, I saw in a museum in North Clark Street Wirtz' two huge dogs, which
in his Andersonville days he used to sic on the prisoners. They were two terrible bitches, one weighing 185,
the other 190 pounds, with incisors that would scare you
to death.

Holÿ had a checkered career that included herding sheep for butchers in
St. Louis, and stirring the cauldrons
in a candy factory; he was also a coal-
miner, waiter, brakeman on the railroad, and just before the Chicago fire
he was a barber. He settled down as a
clerk in a wholesale grocery and found
time to get married and sire five
children, of whom Edward became a professional baseball player. One chapter in his life was devoted to pros-
pecting for oil, near Hannibal, Missouri.

I worked at the drilling machine. We expected that
any day a rich stream of oil would gush forth from the
ground and bring us a fortune or at least prosperity.
But we drilled down to 900 feet, and nothing doing. But
one day it blew. The drill, the augers 4 and a half inches thick, all flew up in the air, and suddenly there
was a stream of fluid gushing upwards about 40 feet.
Alas, it was not oil. We hit a strong hot spring and
not the oil we so ardently yearned for. It was no ordinary water, but water with a sure mineral odor to it;
when you drank it, it made a revolution in your stomach
like some laxative. People started coming from the nearby town with pitchers to fetch the water--but everybody
only came once . . . so I lost my job and went back to
Mr. Trescher, where I polished carriage wheels with sand-
paper and helped painting them.

THE FARMER'S FRONTIER

As the farmer's frontier moved westward, many farmers moved several
times to newer lands. J. Švehla was
among them; he was also a surveyor.

Source: Abstracted from F. J. Swehla,
"Bohemians in Central Kansas," Col-
lections, Kansas State Historical
Society, Topeka, 1913-1914.

Švehla grew up in Iowa, where his family was among
the earliest Czech settlers. As immigrants of all times,
the Czechs also adjusted English words to their own
language. Thus they called a sod house "soddy" or drnǎk,
a log cabin "loksǎk." Švehla recalled his first home, a
combination of both: "Father dug a hole in a hill on
land bought from the government at one dollar and twenty-
five cents per acre. Over the hole, which was about
10 x 12 feet, father built our home. He arranged logs
on the four sides with three beams for girders to hold
the dirt roof. There was a door and one window on one
end."
Švehla became part of the westward movement of the
farmer's frontier: "On May 18, 1868, I married Miss
Anna Kuchta in church at Spillville, Iowa. I put my
bride into a prairie schooner, a brand new covered wagon
drawn by two yoke of oxen, leading a caravan westward
over the swamps and prairies of Iowa into Eastern Dakota.
We arrived in Saline county, Nebraska, located and sur-
veyed claims for many new settlers in Nebraska, mostly
in Solone county, and helped to build up one of the best
Bohemian settlements in the State."
But his road to success was not all that simple.
Twice a prairie fire destroyed his property; he earned
a living as a teacher. Then he moved to Wilson, Kansas,
where he started all over again. His farm was on the
path over which cowboys drove herds of cattle from Texas
to the railheads of Kansas during the era of the Cattle
Kingdom. He became the victim of the long standing ani-
mosities between cowboys resenting farmers' fences, and
farmers objecting to the thousands of cattle ruining
their fields. Another time grasshoppers destroyed his
crops. Švehla had admirable determination. His per-
severance finally paid off; he became one of the prosperous Czechs in Kansas; he was a county surveyor and
later a judge. By placing advertisements in the Czech
papers East of the Mississippi, he attracted many settlers to Kansas.

THE WESTWARD TRECK

Czech farmers were searching for a
rural settlement, where they could
establish an agricultural community. True to their fashion, they
formed an organization called "Česká
osada" or "Czech Settlement." About
500 members signed up in Chicago,
Cleveland, Detroit, Milwaukee and
elsewhere. The leaders could not
decide between Dakota Territory
and the recently created state of
Nebraska, and the group ended up
settling in both. Thus in 1869 the
great westward treck got under way;
the first section in July, the second
in October.

Source: Ružena Rosická, Dějiny Čechů
v Nebrasce, Omaha, 1928.

They went by train to Sioux City, Iowa, which had
at that time a thousand inhabitants and was the end of
the line. Then they continued on wagons for a hundred
more miles. They expected to go by ship, but navigation
was already suspended until next spring. Josef Šedivý,
who had a grocery in Chicago, was better off financially
than the rest, and besides a load of food, he also had
a pair of large oxen and a new Schuttler wagon. Noll
and Vampula together had enough to buy in Chicago a new
wagon and a pair of young oxen. Holeček and Gregor worked
in Chicago, but they had not been paid; the former had
to leave behind 90 dollars and Gregor 70 dollars in un-
paid wages. They asked the Czech lawyer Frank Pratl to
collect the wages for them, but each received only 25
dollars, which was all their capital to start a farm.
Holeček also brought along food, and when he and Gregor
paid their share of the communal expenses, each were
left with ten dollars.

They travelled over deserted, burnt prairies, with
no sign of a habitation or of a living soul. Their first
Nebraskan dish was a soup made of prairie chicken. The
leader was Josef Šedivý; Krupička functioned as the dri-
ver of the first team. They both left their families
temporarily in Sioux City. This group arrived in Niobrara on November 2, 1869. The women and Holeček's son
walked all the way; the men were in charge of the teams.
Members of the Šedivý and Krupička families started out
on November 18, 1869 for Yankton [Dakota] and arrived

on November 21; there they lived together in a deserted
hut on a certain farm. They had to wait for the river
to freeze in order to cross over to the other side.
They finally arrived in Niobrara on December 17, 1869.
By that time the fortune of Šedivý had shrunk to a mere
five dollars.

The group suffered considerable losses. In Sioux
City they had placed all their belongings in the warehouse of the Charles and Tuttle Company. The day they
left, a group of soldiers were bivouacked in the warehouse; they were recruits on their way to Fort Sully in
the Dakotas. The soldiers were drunk and stole, sold
or ruined everything in the settlers' trunks. Šedivý
lost 246 dollars worth of things, the rest all together
about 239. The police could not do a thing with the
soldiers, and the suit that Šedivý brought later, had
no results.

In the spring of 1870 still a third section of pioneers started out from Chicago, under the leadership of
Václav Randa and the lawyer František Partl . . . mostly with their families. The Brabenec family lost two
children, they were killed by enemy redskins the very
first day on their new land.

EDUCATION IN NEBRASKA

By the 1920's there were in Nebraska
eight Czech male professors at the
University of Nebraska; 29 male and 40
female high school teachers; an equal
number (11) were male and female prin-
cipals or supervisers. But the beginnings of Czech teachers were no bed of
roses, and the pay scanty, more so for
the women than for the men. The following excerpt deals with Nebraska,
but it could apply to any other early
settlement of immigrants.

Source: Rose Rosicky, A History of
Czechs (Bohemians) in Nebraska,
Omaha, 1929.

The first public-school teacher of Czech birth, of
whom we have record, and he undoubtedly is the first,
is Frank Znamenáček, a pioneer of Saline County, still
living in Crete. He was born in Maçovice, Benešov,
Tábor, and came to Cincinnati, Ohio, in 1862, attending
school there a short time. During 1863 and 1864 he was
employed by the government as baker, baking bread and
crackers for the soldiers. He came to Saline County in
1869. In 1867 . . . the Czechs in Saline County, at
Joseph Jindra's instigation, formed a Reading Society.
Later a little log building was erected on Joseph Jelinek's farm, 14x16x6, with three windows and a door.
It was built by the settlers in two days. Seats and a
table of boards were provided and Jindra taught in
Czech. The Reading Society met there also. In 1869
Znamenáček began to teach in English, although he
taught during the first three months without text books;
they were that long in coming. At that time the school
belonged to District No. 3, which was organized October
6, 1868, and covered a large territory, twenty-six sec-
tions of land. Later it was subdivided, and a better
building, still standing in Big Blue Precinct, was erected. Znamenáček was succeeded by Miss Mary Nedela (later Mrs. Kubíček), Mrs. E. F. Stephens, Mr. E. F. Stephens (for many years a prominent nurseryman in that vicinity), Vinc. Dvořák, and others. The women received
$25.00 salary per month, the men $40.00.

THE CHICAGO FIRE

Sunday evening, October 8, 1871, the Great Chicago Fire broke out; it was caused allegedly by Mrs. O'Leary's cow, which kicked over a lamp onto the straw of its barn. The 40 year old city had by then 300,000 inhabitants, of whom one third became homeless. Several Czechs left us their detailed descriptions of the conflagration, of people, horses, cattle, dogs, cats and rats running in confusion, of people going insane and committing suicide, of pickpockets and looters, even of several cases of arson [!] on the third day of the tragedy; under martial law, arsonists were shot on the spot. The fire broke out close to the heart of Chicago's Prague. There had been no rain for weeks, and the wooden homes, factories and sidewalks were an easy prey for the flames.

In the following excerpts we hear a new theory about the start of the fire from Alexander Purer; an opinion how much of the tragedy could have been prevented, had the Chicago firemen been able to read the mind of Jan Kralovec, and finally the activities during the fire of everpresent Eduard Holý, who - according to the consensus of several diarists - saved most of the Czech quarter by diverting the fire from their streets.

Source: Rudolf Bubeníček, comp. <u>Dějiny Čechů v Chicagu</u>, Chicago, 1939.

Alexander Purer's theory:

The O'Leary's barn had a window opening on the back yard of Krenek's Czech tavern. . . . At Krenek's tavern there was a small dance hall, where on the fateful evening there was a party, organized as was the custom by the tavern-keeper. After dancing the young folks used to go out to the yard to cool off and they did not behave like angels. . . . some of the frolicsome dancers could have carelessly thrown a burning cigarette or cigar into the open window. Several of

our people considered the possibility that the fire had
started this way, but it was kept for obvious reasons
in great secrecy. If the rest of the people had heard
of it, it could have brought down their wrath on our
nationality. Before that ever happened, the dangerous
thought was overshadowed by the story about the cow,
and that was the end of it.

Jan Kralovec's opinion:

I do not want to repeat the old story about the
start of the fire, about that famous cow, who was allegedly milked for the second time that night . . . how
in anger and sorrow over human injustice she kicked the
pail and the lamp. In a few moments the barn was in
flames, then the small wooden house, and the fire was
extending in all directions. To the east was the Gymnastic Union of Sokol, to the west the church of St.
Václav, and to the south the Czecho-American Sokol, each
only two blocks from the burning hut. I was at the time
of the start of the fire at the Gymnastic Union of Sokol,
where the Czech theatre presented the play "The Orphan
of Lowood." After the first act I saw through the window the flames shooting high up, and people already
started running around. I did not delay either and ran
to the fire. On Taylor Street, the homes of the Czechs
Jan Kolář, Tehla and others were already ablaze. The
fire was spreading fast, because the sparks and burning
chips were flying to the two story buildings around,
and the wooden roofs easily ignited from the fiery rain.
The firemen were already there and they directed streams
of water into the burning buildings through the windows.
In my opinion, however, the streams of water should have
been hitting the roofs and kept them soaked. Because I
did not know enough English, my mental advice was of no
use. Who knows if they would have listened to me even
if I had told them so in perfect English. But till this
day, I am of the opinion that my way of handling it
would have limited the fire to only the southern side
of Taylor Street. Their way, in a few minutes the
flames were blazing on the other street and it also was
all aflame.

Eduard Holý's action:

In our Union that night there was a theatrical performance. I was also a great dramatic artist. I had
an excellent voice--to prompt--and my kingdom was the
prompter's booth in front of the stage. How we got out
when the cries "fire" sounded, how I squeezed myself
free of my burrow under the stage, I no longer remember.
. . . Fellow-countryman Lojza Uher had a small hardware
store at Canal and Forquer and he had a small horse and

wagon. With his wagon he kept transporting the belongings of other Czechs to some safe spot; when he returned
from one of these hauls, he found that while he was sav-
ing the property of others, the fire engulfed his own.
There was no way to save anything, and so Uher's little
dwelling and shop with everything in it disappeared in
a sea of flames, spreading wider and wider. On Canal
and Taylor was Vojta Vaška's tavern in Haisman's house.
That one did not burn down, and that is where we had our
center and our headquarters. There the Sokols congrega-
ted, shared the news and decided where their help was
most needed and consulted on what to do. Across the
street from the Union was a wooden bin for coal, which
caught fire, and the flames started spreading and lick-
ing the back wall of the Union. Vojta noticed it first
and cried out: Boys, our Union is on fire! . . . We
went closer to see what we could do. On Forquer we saw
a fire engine without firemen. The machinist was there.
. . . That fire engine did us a good service. With Sol-
tys and the machinist and with the help of some other
people, we pulled the engine to Beach and Taylor Streets,
plugged it into the hydrant, the machinist started the
motor, and in a while a stream of water gushed forth.
That first stream of water was so powerful that it swept
the cap off the head of the inexperienced young man who
was holding the hose. That amateur fireman was I. Soon
my cap was replaced by old Mr. Šeda, who had a hat business on Canal Street, and who had seen how I came to lose
my cap in the service of fatherland and nation. Meanwhile we were heroically pouring the water into the
place beyond our hall and on its roof, even on the statue of Libuše, that stood on it, and that was how we
saved the hall.

THE CREED OF THE FREETHINKERS

Source: Hlas jednoty svobodomysl-
nÿch (Voice of the Freethinkers'
Union), Iowa City, Iowa, June 3, 1872.

1. We see, believe and comprehend that everything
that exists, grows and lives is directed by certain
laws or intelligence.
2. We see, believe and comprehend that in all di-
versity things are mutually related through natural law.
3. We see, believe and comprehend that this mutual-
ity is graduated, as lower organisms combine and create
higher ones.
4. We see, believe and comprehend that the most
complex and hence most perfect culmination of this development is the human being.
5. We see, believe and comprehend that man's highest
emanation is his spirit, that is his mind and will,
which is called "I".
6. We see, believe and comprehend that man by himself is powerless and incomplete, and individuals are
called upon to combine their minds and their wills into
higher entities, first into small communities, then into larger ones, and ultimately into a unity of all mankind; we call this self-conscious entity Great Mankind,
whom all should serve as the only Lord on earth.
7. We see, believe and comprehend that the earth
is but one member of a higher unit, the solar system.
8. We surmise, that this solar system is also but
a member of a still higher unit, and that any other possible units form one body, which we call the universe.
9. We believe that every creature has a purpose as
a member of the universe, and this purpose is called
universality.
10. We believe and comprehend that everything has
an awareness of this universality, and we term this
religion.
11. We believe and comprehend that unconscious creatures fulfill their purpose by existing, growth and life,
and we term this natural religion.
12. We feel, believe and comprehend that conscious
creatures are liberated through their consciousness,
hence they should voluntarily fulfill their purpose,
and that is conscious or free religion.
13. We call the greatness of the universe harmony,
the laws of the universe as the objects of cognizance
truth. . . .
14. The devotion of one member of the universe to
another is love, its conscious exercise is justice; the
process of learning about the laws of the universe is
science, and the imitation of universal harmony is art.

AN OPERA HOUSE IN MANITOWOC

In 1884 the Czechs at the small town
of Manitowok, Wisconsin, decided to
enlarge their club hall that had served
as meeting place, ballroom and theatre.
No sooner did the news get around about
the ambitious cultural project, than
the townspeople contributed a plot of
land for the purpose. The old hall was
moved to the new site and transformed
into a magnificent stage, the curtain
bearing the likeness of the National
Theatre in Prague. No expense was
spared to build an Opera House, that
solemnly opened its doors on November 1,
1885.

Source: Ruth Pech Gillespie, "The Bohemian Opera House at Manitowoc," Manitowoc County Historical Society, Occu-
pational Monograph 24, 1974 Series,
Manitowoc, Wisconsin; "The Czech Opera
Hall in Manitowoc, Wisconsin", Kvĕty
Americké, April 13, 1887.

Of simple Victorian style, the Opera House was a
dream fulfilled. Constructed of natural brick, its fron-
tage measured sixty by a hundred fifty feet and was
three and a half stories high. Carved over the front
was the proud inscription "Česko-Slovanská Lípa Opera,
1886." On the nights of performances, a brightly lighted canopy was a veritable beacon to all, who came from
near and far to bow to Thalia. They arrived with their
horses and buggies, later in their motor cars; but in
the winter they still had to depend on horses and cut-
ters, with people bundled up like Eskimoes in long coats,
scarfs, caps pulled down over their ears, and hot bricks
at their feet, all covered with a fur cutter robe.
The theatre was constructed ingeniously, with a slo-
ping floor removable for dances. Orchestra seats, uphol-
stered in a medium shade of green plush, took up the
front third of the auditorium. These were the highest
priced seats ($2.50) in the house; the rest were veneered
maple. There were six boxes--a vantage point for chap-
erones at dances, and a gallery (50¢). Wall bracketed
lights and a huge crystal chandelier with thirty-six gas
lights provided illumination. The fly gallery over the
stage was off limits to all but stage-hands; I recall my
brother telling me, how he and his friend climbed the
forbidden wall ladder and lost their awe watching the

magician make his charming assistant "disappear" from
his trunk!

The late Stephen Krianik managed the Opera House until 1901, then my father, Stephen Pech took over for the
next twenty years. There was also a library room in the
Opera, a parlor for the ladies as well as a kitchen and
dining room. A door connected conveniently to a saloon,
that served free lunch. Sliced bologna, cheese, tiny
dried salted and smoked fish, crackers and Bohemian car-
away rye bread were always available to the patrons. Women and children were never present in the bar-room. Only after the theatre were we allowed to snoop around the
place, inserting pennies in the vending machine for the
not too fresh salted peanuts.

The Opera House served several purposes. Balls,
monthly dances, and masquerades were held there regularly.
It was the scene of the dancing classes and of high school
graduations; the Monday Music Club met there, as did the
Sokol, which performed its gymnastic pageants, boys in
white uniforms, girls in their full black bloomers and
white middies. For the children, the annual Christmas
party was the crowning event of the year. Just before
the grand parade march, the enormous tree was tilted to
the ground, spilling its spoils; children were scrambling
over its boughs and stripping them of goodies. In a few
moments their harvest was complete. Pockets bulging with
candy and hands clutching fruit, the disheveled youngsters
dashed to friends and relatives to exhibit their bounty.
Emma Dent recalled: "I ran with the mob one year, and
wound up flat on the floor, under a pile of kids. When
I finally got out, all I had to show for my trouble was
a piece of pink striped ribbon candy. To top it all, my
mother scolded me for joining in the rough and tumble."

The theatre was also rented to Elks, Home Guard, and
other organizations for dances. In later years, there
was a motor car exhibit held there, with models of Oak-
lands, Maxwells, Fords and Wintons. The poultry fanciers
moved in for their annual exhibit. The sawdust covered
floors were lined with rows of tables, each holding cages
of fine specimens of pure-bred chickens. Brilliantly
feathered high-crowned roosters strutted arrogantly within the confines of wire cages. Their clarion calls ech-
oed and re-echoed in the lofty hall, reminding the spectators of the true mission of the premises. Great white
hens with queer looking downy legs scratched about crack-
ling contentedly, their beady eyes studying the judges,
as though soliciting their votes!

The "Bohemian Girl" played the Opera House when my
oldest sister Mildred was a very little girl. She was
to be Princess Arline, stolen by the gypsies. She cried
and cried; finally they had to get Vlasta Nespor to take
her place. Years later, when I was about four or five
years old, the "Bohemian Girl" played again, and this

time my father loaned me. The gypsy king lifted me in
his arms and went on stage, where he held me while he
sang his solo.

Stock companies often performed in the Opera House.
My sister saw "Uncle Tom's Cabin" twenty-eight times, a
record I could never match. Swarms of children attended
the matinees. Other plays I recall were musical come-
dies, like "Chin Chin," "Lilac Domino," "Bringing up Father" and the "Katzenjammer Kids." My brother Edwin told
me that he was once standing in the wings back stage
with a cigarette in his mouth; as the chorus girls were
entering the stage, one of them reached for his cigarette, took a puff, put it back, and joined the chorus
line. Years later Edwin recognized her in a scene in a
movie. She was Barbara Stanwyck.

Newspaper notices were carried in the Manitowoc
Herald, as were the reviews. Newspaper editors always
received complimentary tickets for their wives and themselves. "Sammy the Opera House dog was there," they reported once. This was our Spitz, a born extrovert and
theatre goer.

The amateur theatre group, called the "Ochotnik"
(amateur actors and actresses) had a good reputation.
Frank and Joe Cerney, Karel Sindelár, Vítek the tailor,
the two Sladkys, Anna Skála--they drew crowds from all
over the county. All monies were sent to Bohemia along
with profits from food sales, especially during the struggle for a free Czechoslovakia. People would come from
Melnik, Larabee and Francis Creek to see the "Ochotnik"
melodramas at the Opera House, or to attend a Bohemian
farce with singing and dancing ["Bartered Bride?"].

"YEARNING FOR THE LORD'S TEMPLE"

The following poem was written by Jan
Štepán Brož (1865-1919), a Czech Catholic priest in Nebraska, who was also an anthropologist interested in
the American Indians. The free
translation is by E. Žižka. The
poem reflects the falling away of
the Catholics from the Church and
the dichotomy between the Catholics
and the freethinkers.

Source: Ernest Žižka, Czech Cultural
Contributions. Lisle, Illinois, 1937.

Still there were times when Jakub's brow did darken
'Twas on Sunday mornings that his soul would harken
to some far distant nonexistent ringing;
it felt as if his heart would leave him,
and as a pigeon homing
so his own soul in longing
sought now the sainted blessed premise of the Lord.
. . . .
What would he give if with his wife in prayer
he now could kneel before the Blessed Sacrament;
to honor God intoning old Czech chorals,
to listen to a sermon in his own native tongue.

He kept his faith, forever he shall keep it
as a dear heritage from ages past;
but his own progeny, 'tis they that engage his mind now:
What will they do when leaving their native home?
Who will then aid them when human passions smoulder?
. . . .
It is hard to bring up children without that faith,
and even now when indifferent and lukewarm neighbors
bide here; -- how many of them honor
the Lord's appointed day?
Forsooth, most all of them now dabble in the scathing
embittered Free Thought way.

Announce, declare, affirm you old Catholic faith;
be unabashed to tell them that your way is to pray.
And though they fling derision, denounce your sacred hope,
poke fun at priesthood, temple keep on my lonesome soul!

To them our dearest Lord's way has long ceased to be a call;
now they would rather listen to apostatic growl.
And if in some a glimmer,
a spark of conscience be left,
shamefaced his head is lowered, his heart of truth bereft.

AMERICA ADOPTS DVOŘÁK'S MUSIC

Composer Antonín Dvořák was director of the National Conservatory of
Music in New York from 1892 to 1895.
In 1893 he composed his offering to
America, "From the New World." Its
premiere at Carnegie Hall in December of 1893 received rave reviews.

Source: New York Herald, December 16, 1893.

Dr. Antonín Dvořák, the famous Bohemian composer
and director of the National Conservatory of Music, dow-
ered American art with a great work yesterday, when his
new symphony in E minor 'From the New World' was played
at the second Philharmonic rehearsal in Carnegie Music
Hall. The day was an important one in the musical history of America. It witnessed the first performance of
a noble composition.
It saw a large audience of usually tranquil Americans enthusiastic to the point of frenzy over a musical
work and applauding like the most excitable "Italianissi-
mi" in the world.
The work was one of heroic proportions. And it was
one cast in the art form which such poet-musicians as
Beethoven, Schubert, Schumann, Mendelsohn, Brahms and
many other 'glorious ones of the earth' have enriched
with the most precious outwelling of his musical imagination.
And this new symphony by Antonín Dvořák is worthy
to rank with the best creations of these musicians whom
we have just mentioned. Small wonder that the listeners
were enthusiastic. The work appealed to their sense of
the aesthetically beautiful by its wealth of tender,
pathetic, fiery melody; by its rich harmonic clothing;
by its delicate, sonorous, gorgeous, ever varying instru-
mentation.
And it appealed to the patriotic side of them. For
had not Dr. Dvořák been inspired by the impressions
which this country had made upon him? Had he not translated these impressions into sounds, into music? Had
they not been assured by the composer himself that the
work was written under the direct influence of a serious
study of the national music of the North American Indians?
Therefore, were they not justified in regarding the composition, the first fruits of Dr. Dvořák's musical gen-
ius since his residence in this country, as a distinctive
American work of art?

THE FIRST CZECH WOMAN DOCTOR

Anna Nováková was the wife of a tailor. When the doctor could not save
her baby from dying of diphtheria,
she made up her mind to become a doctor. Well in her twenties, she had
to go through studies of grammar
school and high school, before gain-
ing admission to Bennett's Medical
College in Chicago. She became a doctor in 1895 at the age of 31, the
first Czech woman doctor in the United States.

Source: Rudolf Bubeníček., comp. Dějiny
Čechů v Chicagu, Chicago, 1939.

When she started practicing medicine, Dr. Nováková
ran head on into deep-rooted prejudices against women
and their aspirations for emancipation not only among
the simple folk, but also among the educated ones, even
among her colleagues. She caused a storm; even Dr. Fran-
tisek Jirka, a kind man and popular in the Czech colony,
objected. He had a consulting room in Mrázek's apothe-
cary shop on Ashland Avenue next to 18th Street. But he
refused to keep his hours, when the pharmacist allowed
Dr. Nováková to practice there and hang her shingle on
the door of the pharmacy. The doctor had a good reputation and a prospering practice and he certainly was not
opposed to his lady colleague for material reasons, only
because of old fashioned prejudices. Initial difficulties did not deter Dr. Nováková; if anything, they spurred
her on to study further. In 1900 she carried on studies
at the University of Illinois and in 1906 she enriched
her knowledge in Prague at the clinic of professor Dr.
Maixner in nervous disorders and of professor Dr. Pavlík
in female disorders.

By 1897 Novák closed his tailor shop in the center
of the city; they purchased a house at 1420 18th Street,
where Novák plied his trade for a few more years, but
after that he was only driving Dr. Nováková on her rounds
of housecalls.

CZECHS IN POLITICS

Czechs were slow in getting into
local, state or federal politics. Originally they voted Republican because
they had admired Lincoln, but gradually
they switched to the Democrats. The
present excerpt refers to Wisconsin,
where Czechs voted Republican during
the era of reformer "Fighting Bob" La
Follette; he was U. S. Congressman from
1884 to 1890 and despite breaking with
the party machine was elected governor
in 1901.
    Charles Jonáš was the moving spirit
behind the incorporation of the Czech
library in Racine, Wisconsin, in 1861;
see document above.

Source: V. V. Vlach, "Our Bohemian Population," Proceedings, Wisconsin Historical Society, Madison, 1902.

    Aside from an exceedingly personal interest which
the Bohemians always take in every election, their duties to their homes and families have overshadowed any
temptation to become political leaders or conspicuous
public characters. Thus far in this state they have
proven themselves content with gradual financial success
as laborers, farmers, mechanics, and business men. They
follow admirably the wise saying that "an unwise thirst
for public employment is the worst of social maladies."
Of course, if either of the two great political parties
recognizes them with an appointive office, they take
great pride in the fact; or, when one of them is elected
to an office, he always, so far as I know, tries to perform its duties honestly. I am still looking for a Bohemian-American who, whether appointed or elected to an
office, proved himself false or dishonest. It may be
said of the Bohemians that, just as Hollanders are and
always were unswerving Republicans, so the Bohemians
were always loyal Democrats; but in recent years many of
them are changing their political views and are joining
the ranks of the Republicans. Let scorn or wit exhaust
their sneers and jibes, one fact must be admitted and
cannot be truthfully denied of Bohemians--that as "Mug-
wumps" they have always exerted themselves for something
higher and nobler than mere official patronage, and they
cannot be accused of office-begging. This alone gives
them a right to respect, and in it can be discerned a
principle of political action, which should be an inspiring

and elevating force in a government like our own.

Among the few men who have held positions of political prominence, and have been more or less influential in shaping the political choice of the Bohemians in America, was the lamented Charles Jonas of Racine, who, serving this country as consul to Germany, came to an untimely death. With deep affection for and trust in his own people, he made it his life-work to try to better their condition. He was recognized as the Bohemian authority of this country. His close application to literature and journalism, and his own ambitious efforts, undermined his health. He was editor of the _Slavie_, and author of various useful books; among these were translations of American laws and the constitution, and English-Bohemian and Bohemian-English dictionaries--books which may be found in almost every Bohemian home.

In conclusion, I will only add that the Bohemians do not pretend to be better than any other of the many nationalities that establish their homes in this state; but I do claim that they try their best to be good American citizens, and they only ask from their American fellow-citizens charitable indulgence for their imperfections and deficiencies. In a decade or two there will no longer be Germans, Bohemians, Irish, Hollanders, Poles or other foreign elements, but one great, invincible, and liberty-loving American nation. The many nationalities that now occupy the United States will only live in history. And the Bohemians, like others, try to bequeath to their children and descendants an honest and untarnished name, so that in after years they need not be ashamed of their Bohemian ancestors; but may with pride own that they are Americans of Bohemian descent.

THE COUNCIL OF HIGHER EDUCATION

The Czechs have ever considered
themselves the nation of John Amos Comenius (1592-1670), the progressive
educator of the 17th century. He was
the bishop of the Czech Brethren; he
declined Harvard's offer to become president of the college. He advocated universal education for both sexes in the
native tongue, not in Latin. In Orbis
Pictus and Schola Ludus he recommended
progressive methods of teaching. The
Czechs are proud of the fact that they
established the first university in
Central Europe, Charles University,
founded in 1348. In the spirit of this
tradition, the education of their children was foremost in the minds of Czech
immigrants.
The Matice vyššího vzdělání, or
Council of Higher Education, founded in
1902 in Iowa, described below, later
moved to Chicago and has facilitated
the higher education of hundreds of
Czech and later also Slovak immigrants
and their children; it is still in existence.

Source: Nan Mashek, "Bohemian Farmers
in Wisconsin," Charities, December 3, 1904.

In the matter of higher education, the Bohemians
of Kewaunee county have a remarkably good record. Within the last twenty-five years the local high school has
sent to college fifty-nine young men and women and of
these thirty were Bohemians. It is plain, then, that
there is no lack of ambition in the children of our pioneers, and this ambition is upheld and fostered by progressive Bohemians of the West. Two years ago a council of higher education was organized at Cedar Rapids,
Iowa, which, in the words of its constitution, is "to
encourage the Bohemian youth to acquire higher education,
to inform our people concerning the manner in which they
may secure such education for their children, and the
advantages which various educational institutions afford,
and to aid promising students, who lack the material
means necessary to higher education, by honor-loans,
without interest."
The society was organized mainly through the efforts of W. F. Severa, a prominent Bohemian of Cedar

Rapids, and Professor Simek of Iowa University. To put
the project in motion, Mr. Severa subscribed $2,500, a
sum which has been so liberally contributed to by Bohemian societies and individuals that in the two years
the society has been able to loan much more. Though in
1903-4 there were seven students at various western
universities and this year the number has been increased
to twelve, it is hoped that as the fund increases, both
by contributions and repaid loans, the society will be
able to broaden its scope.

The movement is further supported by another, the
aim of which is to establish Bohemian libraries in the
larger Bohemian communities. The public library of Milwaukee is to install one hundred books on history, literature, biography, fiction and science and the Free
Library Commission of Wisconsin is considering the pur-
chase of two sets of books, seventy-five in each, to be
used as traveling libraries in the thickly populated
districts of the state. In addition to these libraries,
there is to be another of about a hundred books at the
University of Nebraska, and a second traveling library
under the management of the council of higher education.
Mr. Severa voices the ambition of progressive Bohemian-
Americans when he says: "We want our young men and women to enter American colleges and to work hand in hand
with Americans on the path of progress, but we want
them at the same time to respect the land of their fathers, to know their language and to be informed concerning their history and literature."

In the country the assimilation of Bohemians is
not a problem which offers difficulties. The public
school is everywhere so potent an Americanizer that it
alone is adequate.

CZECHS IN CHICAGO IN THE EARLY 1900's

Chicago was the second largest Czech
city after Prague. Around the turn
of the century about 50,000 Czech immigrants lived there. Of the close
to 120,000 first and second generation Czechs in Illinois, most lived
in various colonies like Česká Kali-
fornie and Pilsen in Chicago, starting to spread out from Berwyn to
Cicero and later to Riverside. The
writer of this report, Dr. Alice G.
Masaryk, was a social worker in the
University of Chicago Settlement.
She was the daughter of Professor
Thomas Masaryk, who became the cre-
ator of Czechoslovakia in 1918. His
wife was Charlotte Garrigue of Brooklyn, thus all the children were half
American, half Czech. Masaryk took
his wife's maiden name for his, and
became officially Thomas Garrigue
Masaryk, or T. G. M., the only man
in the country known by his initials.

Source: Alice G. Masaryk, "The Bohemians in Chicago," Charities, December 3, 1904.

I.

Half a century has passed since Bohemians first
crossed the ocean, and after a long and dreaded journey
and much uncertainty, settled down in Chicago, which was
then scarcely more than a large village on the Lake shore
in the endless prairie. . . .

When they decide to leave the village or town they
were born in, the pain of parting gives life to a new,
strong love for the new country, the unknown yet longed-
for home. And they come with the intention of becoming
American citizens.

Even by a conservative element, the Bohemians are
considered desirable immigrants. The number of illiter-
ates is small; in the country districts they make good
farmers; they are clever handworkers in the towns. The
last is of special interest for Chicago, and is borne out
by the fact that of 9,591 Bohemians who came to the United States in 1902-3, 2,609 were skilled workmen. The
United States census of 1900 shows that 75.8 per cent of
the Bohemians live in the Northwest, [Middle West] which
is prevailingly agricultural. Of the Bohemians who came
over in 1903 only 1.2 per cent were illiterate--a pro-

portion exceeded only by the Finnish and Scandinavian immigrants of this year [and lower than the overall American illiteracy rate].

The change the Bohemians undergo in crossing the ocean and settling down in Chicago is a radical one. From the Austrian monarchy under which the Catholic church has been indirectly forced upon them, they come into a republic where freedom of religion is acknowledged. From villages and little, old towns, they come into the rushing city of Chicago. Their inward, often unconscious, store of principles and thoughts, superstitions and prejudices, has to be revised because it has been revolutionized. Sometimes the revision is swept away by the revolution.

What intense mental work it requires to distinguish the wisdom of ages crystallized into tradition from an organic prejudice--faith from superstition. Very, very few can do so much and therefore the hardship, the unevenness of the first generation of Bohemians.

The simple, gentle manners of a Bohemian peasant and artisan have to undergo a period of change through the distrust accorded all strangers and the imitation of those **beati possidentes** that inherited their traditions and manners from other ancestors. This queer mixture in the period of changing does not raise sympathy in those who, because they see only the surface, cannot understand and therefore cannot love.

The Bohemians at home have a strong family life. A married son or daughter remains under the same roof with the aged parents, who retire into a quiet nook, where they enjoy their flaxen-haired, brown-eyed grandchildren. This trait, though modified, continues in Chicago. On a Sunday afternoon, the Eighteenth street car is filled with families, scrubbed, brushed and starched-up, bound for some festival hall to have a good time.

The Bohemian housekeepers know how to get great results from small means, which is most valuable for the poorer class and shows in the red and glossy cheeks of the children. On the other hand, the heavy food (pork with dumplings, for instance, is very common, and with it the usual glass of beer) produces those of full forms without corresponding strength, so general among the well-to-do citizens.

The Bohemians are capable of being amalgamated quickly. They learn the language easily, they give work for which even under competition, they can demand decent wages; they take an interest in politics.

II.

Two pages, large sheets of the daily paper _Svornost_ lie before me, covered with small print, giving the names of Bohemian clubs, societies, and lodges in Chicago. The Catholic press gives another long list of Catholic lodges,

Catholic clubs. This fever for organization is typical
of the Bohemians in Chicago. . . .

The social life among the Bohemians is very much a-
live. There are dances, concerts, theatrical performances. Since the Columbian Exposition a company of professional actors has resided in Pilsen, who on Sunday
evenings play before a full house in the large hall,
Thalia.

Besides the tendency to avail themselves of the un-
accustomed freedom, other factors enter into the social
life, such as the rivalry between the Catholics and Freethinkers, the rivalry of individuals, and the indirect
economic interest. A new settler finds customers in the
club or lodge he joins. This can be reduced ad absurdum,
when, for instance, all the grocers from the district
meet in the same club with the same intention. The educational element is of great importance. I was struck
by the cleverness and efficiency with which the Bohemian
women conduct their meetings. The men gain here a training for political life.

Other than these mutual benefit organizations, you
will find all kinds of societies especially among the
freethinkers, such as turner (gymnastic) clubs (35),
singing clubs (18), printing clubs (7), bicycle clubs (5),
dramatic clubs (4) and many others.

The Bohemians are born musicians. "Where is the Bohemian who does not love music?" is a cadence in Smetana's
music which says everything. You will find on the West
Side many music schools, many violinists and pianists,
amateurs, besides the professional musicians who have
three unions.

A large park near Dunning, a beautiful garden, is
the Bohemian cemetery. Its beginning belongs to the time
of the separation of the Freethinkers from the Catholic
Church. A Catholic priest refused to bury in the Catholic cemetery a woman who died without a confession, and
the Freethinkers resolved to have a cemetery of their
own. Like the Catechism of Freethinking, this cemetery
proclaims how deeply the roots of Catholic logic and way
of thinking penetrated the Bohemian soul. The great pomp
with which the dead are buried by Freethinkers belongs to
the middle ages, to the shadows of cathedrals. It is
touching to watch the pride with which they love this
piece of American soil. All the thoughts and memories
of their old home, that are so dear to them, seem to be
thought more easily and better in this garden of the dead,
for something died within them when they left their homes.
The pure memory lives as the memory of those who have
left them forever and sleep under that velvety grass, under the brightest autumn leaves and the faithful asters.

CZECH WOMEN IN CIGAR FACTORIES

In the 1860's the first cigar-makers
immigrated from Sedlec, and their
"America Letters" attracted others.
Editor L. J. Palda estimated that in
1873 fully 95% of the Czechs living
in New York were employed in this
field. By 1920 merely 15% of Czech
breadwinners of New York were involved in cigar making. Women and
youngsters were also employed in the
cigar factories.

Source: Jane E. Robbins, "The Bohemian Women in New York," Charities,
December 3, 1904.

The factories in the regions of Seventieth street,
New York, are filled with Bohemian women and girls employed in the making of cigars. When the Bohemians
first came to this country they made the cigars in their
own homes, and cigar-making was classed with tailoring
as one of the tenement-house industries. The introduc-
tion of the suction-table and the bunchmaking machine
ci anged cigar-making into factory work, though a few men
are making the finest grades of cigars by hand.
  The Bohemian girls dread going into the cigar factories. The hygiene is bad, the moral influences are often not of the best, and the work is exhausting. An oc-
casional factory inspector, a little protection from the
law, and even from the labor union is what the workers
have to depend upon to help them gain the chance to earn
their livelihood by healthy toil. The strippers and
bookmakers who get the tobacco ready for the cigarmakers,
work together--sometimes as many as a hundred and fifty
of them--at the end of a room laden with tobacco dust
and heavy with the odor of damp tobacco leaves. The windows are generally kept closed because the tobacco must
not be allowed to become dry.
  The strippers, who know little English and are therefore called "greeners," are paid by the day, and seldom
earn more than five or six dollars a week. They are down
at the bottom of the economic scale and are not admitted
to the cigarmakers' union. . . .
  Many of the cigar-making girls brought up in this
country learn their trade from regular teachers. They
pay for their tuition, and are several weeks in learning
to become bunchmakers or cigarmakers. The bunchmakers
get the tobacco into the shape of a cigar, and the cigar-
makers spread the leaves out on the suction-table and

put the final coverings on. They are both paid by the
thousand cigars, and their wages vary greatly. Some earn
only four or five dollars a week, while others earn
twelve dollars, and sometimes even higher wages. They
are allowed a good deal of latitude as to hours, and often work through the greater part of their lunchtime and
stop work at five o'clock. They work under a considerable
nervous strain, as speed is a first consideration, if
they are to make fair wages. In their hurry many of them
bite off the small ends of the cigars (a pleasant thought
for the smoker) and they sit all day holding bits of tobacco in their mouths.

The light must be good for their work and the heat
of the nearby gas jet adds greatly to the discomfort from
the bad air. The floor and walls of the factory are often dirty and the dressing rooms where clothing is hung,
are simply large closets partly partitioned off from the
main rooms. . . .

To those theorists who look for great progress when
women shall obtain a position of economic independence,
the Bohemian women cigarmakers ought to be an interesting
study. The wife with her quicker fingers often makes
better wages than her husband.

HOME LIFE OF CZECHS IN NEW YORK CITY

When considering the hardships of urban life, one is not surprised to find
that the majority of Czechs preferred
to settle in rural areas. The following description refers to New York City at the beginning of the 20th century.

Source: Jane E. Robbins, "The Bohemian
Women in New York," Charities, December 3, 1904.

Home life among the Bohemians exists under peculiar
difficulties. The mothers work in cigar factories, and
besides the factory work they have the bearing and rear-
ing of children, and sewing, cooking, washing and clean-
ing to do in their homes.

The first result noticed is that everyone keeps
early hours. At nine o'clock on a winter evening, a
block occupied by Bohemian families, is wrapped in slum-
ber, the windows of the houses are dark, and there is almost no one on the street. The working day begins at
half-past five and the tired mothers must have their
children at home and in bed at an early hour.

The most noticeable effect of having the mothers go
to factory is that the ordinary masculine aversion to doing woman's work, is greatly moderated. The boys run
home from their play after school hours to start the
kitchen fire, so that the water may be boiling when
their mothers come home. They make beds and sweep and
clean house. I have known a boy of eleven to acquire
sufficient knowledge of housework so that, at his mother's death, he was able to do all the work for a family
of four. Several times I have come into a home and
found the strong young husband washing, and not at all
embarrassed to be caught at the wash-tub.

The older children, both boys and girls, take care
of the younger ones. They are trained to responsibility
from their earliest youth, and make great gains in both
strength and charm of character. A girl of thirteen often has the care of several younger children, besides
doing much of the housework for the family. A grand-
father or a grandmother, even if very feeble, is a great
addition to the family life in furnishing the adult point
of view in the absence of both parents. A neighbor, too,
in case of sudden emergency, often acts in loco parentis,
and a very motherly person will sometimes mother a whole
neighborhood.

One woman that I knew had ten fine, healthy child-
ren--she had never lost a child--and she had been in fac-

tory the greater part of the time through the twenty-five
years of her married life. The oldest girl was married
and was also at work in a cigar factory, but whenever she
had a few minutes to spare she came to her mother's home
to help with the sewing for those younger brothers and
sisters she had brought up.

The clothes of the children are suitable and are often made with particularly good taste. The Bohemians are
perhaps the cleanest of the poor people in the city and
they struggle manfully against the bad conditions of the
New York tenement houses. They are fortunate in being
intensely musical, and they find great joy in the occa-
sional dance or picnic.

They are a hard-working people, and both the women
and children are often overworked. The girls marry with
the expectation of continuing their hard life in the factory.

"A SONG WITHOUT A MELODY"

Cigar factories held little attraction for most Czechs. Typical are
the reminiscences of old-timer
Štěpánek.

Source: Thomas Čapek, The Čech
(Bohemian) Community of New York,
New York, 1921.

Sixty-odd years of cigar making and not one Čech
manufacturer has risen from the ranks of workers! Thousands of privates, not one employer of labor! A co-operative shop which Čech workmen organized in 1874 went
into the receiver's hands after a short-lived and stormy
existence.

The author asked Mr. Joseph Štěpánek, said to be
the oldest living cigar maker in the city, to set down
in writing his reminiscences. He arrived as a lad of
twelve direct from the factory at Sedlec. As he is now
in his eighty-fifth year, he has been rolling "smokers"
seventy-three years. The observations of this venerable
workman, the author felt, would be exceedingly illumina-
tive. Mr. Štěpánek wrote a modest narrative in which he
told of having witnessed the memorable trial by jury at
Kutná Hora in 1851, of Charles Havlíček, the tribune of
the Čech people. In 1865, he walked with 50 other New
York Čechs in the funeral cortege of Abraham Lincoln.
He described what keen joy he derived as a member of a
New York amateur singing club (he sang tenor); concerning his experiences as a cigar maker he had not a word
to say. "That phase of my life," he explained, "was a
song without a melody."

IN THE STEPS OF PIONEERS

Vojta Beneš was a teacher and jour-
nalist, deeply involved in the movement of American Czechs for independence of their old country. (His brother, Dr. Eduard Beneš, became the
first minister of foreign affairs and
second president of Czechoslovakia.) He
travelled widely among Czech settlements in 1914.

Source: Vojta Beneš, Československá
Amerika v odboji, Praha, 1931.

Kinsmen from the same birthplace or region settled
regularly close by, near to friends and relatives, who
invited them here; thus they formed Czech settlements and
islands in the midst of cities with a million inhabitants
and in the agricultural states. . . . Such settlements
are in New York, Cleveland, Pittsburgh, Chicago, Philadelphia, Baltimore, Omaha, Cedar Rapids, Bridgeport.
That is how Czech Prahas were built (in Nebraska, Minnesota, Oklahoma, Arkansas, Pennsylvania and Texas), several Plzeňs, seven Tábors, Protivín in Iowa, Vodňany and
Písek in the Dakotas, Mělník in Wisconsin, Malín in Ore-
gon, Brno and Slovania in Nebraska. The Moravians founded in Texas their Velehrad, Moravia, Dubina, Polanka,
the Slovaks Slovaktown in Arkansas; Libuše and Kolín appeared right before the war in Louisiana, etc. It is by
no means a singular phenomenon what Dr. Vojan says about
New York, "Whether you come as an immigrant or tourist
to the core of the Czech district, you can easily forget
that you are in America. If it were not for the English
inscriptions on the stores, the Czech talk you hear all
around you and the Czech names on the stores give you the
impression of a Czech town."
When I visited in 1914, just before the war, the
Praha in Oklahoma, the mayor welcomed me--a Czech butcher--
and I heard the greeting of a Czech song played by the
band "When will I see again. . ." The power of national
life was so strong that it could assimilate even fellow
citizens of other nationalities. J. H. Zachar (Minni-
berger) writes in his tale Fog: "Pepito was Italian.
He married, however, a Czech girl, learned Czech, educated his children in the same language and moved in Czech
company." On the western farms it was even more common
that people born in America never learned--English!

THE CZECHOSLOVAK DECLARATION OF INDEPENDENCE IN AMERICA

Just as the British at the twelfth hour of the American Revolution offered to redress all colonial grievances, the Austrian government tried to do the same. To state once and for all that no compromise but independence was their goal, Masaryk and his fellow patriots issued on October 18, 1918 in Washington, D. C., the Czechoslovak Declaration of Independence, in many ways similar to Jefferson's document. Aside from its primary significance, it raised a minor storm because it placed women on equal footing with men in all respects. The first announcement was transmitted to U. S. Secretary of State Lansing. The following is a translation from the original draft.

Source: J. B. Kozák, T. G. Masaryk a vznik Washingtonské deklarace v říjnu 1918, Praha, 1968. The actual letter and enclosure is in Papers relating to the Foreign Relations of the United States, 1918, Supplement I, I:847, National Archives, Washington, D. C.

Mr. Secretary: Washington, October 18, 1918

Political reasons as well as urgent administrative circumstances have led our National Council in accordance with your and Allied approval to assume the title of a government and to publish the enclosed Declaration.

As you, Mr. Secretary, have expressed no wish as to the date of the publication, I assume that it is of no importance, and I am publishing the Declaration today, forced to it by the course of events in Austria-Hungary.

Our government was established thus:
Prime minister and minister of finance: professor Tomáš G. Masaryk; Minister of National Defense: Gen. Dr. Milan R. Štefánik; Minister of Foreign Affairs and of Interior: Dr. Eduard Beneš.

The seat of the government is in Paris.
Please receive . . .

T. G. Masaryk

Excerpts from the enclosed Declaration:

In this solemn moment . . . we, the Czechoslovak National Council, recognized by the Allied and the American governments as the Provisional Government of the Czechoslovak State and Nation . . . proclaim this Declaration of Independence. . . .

We do so because we believe that no people should be
forced to live under an authority they do not recognize,
and because we know and are convinced that our nation can
not develop freely in a sham Hapsburg federation, which
is only a new form of de-nationalizing pressure, under
which we have suffered for the last three hundred years.
We believe that freedom is the first premise of federation. . . .

We make this Declaration based on our historical and
natural rights. We were an independent state since the
seventh century; in 1526 as an independent state consisting of Bohemia, Moravia and Silesia we joined Austria
and Hungary in a defensive union against the Turkish men-
ace. We have never given up voluntarily our rights as an
independent state in this confederation. The Hapsburgs
broke this treaty with our nation by illegally curtailing
our rights and raped the constitution of our state, which
they had bound themselves to respect; therefore we refuse
to remain a part of Austria-Hungary in any form. . . .

We deny the blasphemous statement that the power of
the Habsburg and Hohenzollern dynasties is of divine origin; we refuse to recognize the divine right of kings. . .

We subscribe to and will faithfully exercise the i-
deals of modern democracy that are the same ideals that
our nation has professed for centuries. We accept the A-
merican principles, as established by President Wilson:
the principles of liberated mankind--of true equality of
nations--and the principle that governments derive all
their just powers from the consent of the governed. We,
the nation of Komenský, can not but accept these principles, expressed in the American Declaration of Independence, the principles of Lincoln and the principle of the
Declaration of Rights of Man and Citizen. For these principles our nation had bled in the memorable Hussite Wars
five hundred years ago, for these principles our nation
is bleeding today along with its Allies in Russia, Italy
and France.

The Czechoslovak State will be a republic. In a con-
tinuous effort for progress it will guarantee full freedom of conscience, religion, science, literature and art,
speech, press, assembly and of petition. The church will
be separated from the state. Our democracy will be based
on an equal right to vote; women will be politically, so-
cially and culturally made equal with men. The rights of
minorities will be secured by proportionate representation;
national minorities will enjoy the same rights . . . privileges of the nobility will be abolished.

. . . democracy achieved victory. Humanity will be
reorganized on a democratic basis. The forces of darkness
performed a service by bringing about the victory of light--
the longed for era of humanitarianism is dawning.

We believe in democracy--we believe in liberty, a
liberty ever greater and greater!

THE AMERICANIZATION PROCESS

Nebraska born Rose Rosicky was the
daughter of Omaha editor Jan Rosicky.

Source: Rose Rosicky, A History of
Czechs (Bohemians) in Nebraska, Omaha, 1929.

During the great World War (1914 - 1918) and for
some time after, feeling against foreigners in this
country ran high and the Americanization movement was
begun. At first some of its advocates thought their
first duty lay in eradicating from the hearts and minds
of immigrants all memories of their native land. That
spirit is passing. We know we cannot do that to anyone.
Our immigrants must become good, law-abiding citizens,
but we must not expect that they can put aside what
means so much to them.
When mature or elderly people cross the ocean to settle in a strange country, it is like transplanting old
trees. Such people thereafter are never quite the same
as native inhabitants. They are the span that bridges
over the old generations in Europe with the new in America. Always they think with love and longing of the
dear land of their birth, which is but human and noble.
Did not the great Scottish bard say long ago:

"Breathes there a man with soul so dead,
Who never to himself has said:
This is my own, my native land?"

At the same time they know that our country offers
a better future to them and their descendants. They
love their native land as a man loves his mother; they
love this country as a man loves his wife, who brings
to him children that his line may continue. If they
perform their duty as good citizens and give to the
United States a future race, they have helped fully to
build our splendid commonwealth.
Czech pioneers who came to our beautiful state have
indeed done their part toward changing it from a tree-
less plain to a verdant, fruitful region. In turn, they
have every reason to feel grateful, for Nebraska gave
them an opportunity, even though fraught at first with
hardship, the like of which they could not have even
dreamed about in their small and crowded native land.

"CHANGE NOT THE NAME"

Three quarters of a century after the
Czechs settled the small town of Bohemia on Long Island (1855), political
maneuverings tried to change its name
to Sayville Heights and later to Lidice.
The Czechs still had enough clout to
prevent this. The tempests soon blew
over but not before demonstrations by
young and old testified of the deep
feelings for the name of their town.

Source: A History of Bohemia, Long Island. Bohemia, N. Y., The Centennial
History Book Committee, 1955. Based on
the accounts of Joseph F. Thuma, an old
settler and town historian.

    The younger generation of the village decorated the
whole town one Sunday evening with posters reading as
follows: "We want Bohemia"; "If you don't like the name
Bohemia, move out"; "Keep Bohemia on the map"; "Go back
to where you came from." All were signed "Young people
of the future; we love this name". This was quite a
blow to the politicians and they dropped the entire matter of changing the name.
    In a 1932 issue of the Suffolk County News, a poem
by William Keyes, Bohemia School Principal, was published
as follows:

"CHANGE NOT THE NAME"

In modern days it is not strange
That names, like fashions, often change
The fathers of a former age
Never over names got in rage.
This crossing seas to realms of worth
They had most dear their home of birth.
Then as they reached the red man's trail,
Their stalwart courage did not fail.
But onward through the woods they strode
To find a place for their abode.
Where they bethought to name the place
They chose one not of Indian race,
But gave their new-found home a name
Like unto that from whence they came.
To many thousand far and near
Bohemia's name is held most dear,
Let those who think it is out-of-date
Remove themselves by truck or freight.

It was in the summer of 1942 that a move got under-

way to change the name of the community again, this time
to Lidice. The idea began with an editorial in The New
York Post on June 25th, 1942.

    The editorial read, in part: "We believe the name
of Lidice should be kept alive . . . that some American
town should make itself famous around the world by drop-
ping its present label and renaming itself Lidice." It
suggested that perhaps this gesture would be considered
by Bohemia, Long Island, since this community of Czech
descendants also numbered about 1200, the amount of people Hitler executed in the Czech town of Lidice.

    . . . the idea gained considerable favor at its in-
ception because of the furor of indignation which arose
in all parts of the world . . . some of the foremost citizens of Bohemia favored the idea, arguing that the fine
sentiment showing sympathy with their oppressed Czech
brethren would result in world-wide fame for its own
town and people. On the other hand there proved to be an
unsuspected strong sentiment among the people who more
than half a century ago established in central Long Island a community of Czech people and named it Bohemia. . .

    Shortly thereafter, the opposition to the move being
so great, those in favor of it abandoned the idea and
the community once more regained its composure.

THE SECOND RESISTANCE MOVEMENT IN AMERICA

As during World War I, so twenty years
later the Czechs in America rallied to
the help of their former homeland. Just
before Munich, on September 26, 1938,
65,000 Czechs and Americans demonstrated
against Nazi expansion in Europe. The
Czechs with some foresight started organizing early.

Source: Joseph Martínek, Století Jednoty Č. S. A., Cicero, Illinois, 1955.

Actually the movement for the second liberation of
Czechoslovakia in America started even before the occupation of Austria by the Nazis in the spring of 1938.
Czechs in America, well informed by the American press
and radio, were filled with anxiety about the threatening
German aggression; they started organizing the new action
for the defense of their former homeland, to the liberation of which they had contributed so effectively during
the first world war.

Already on February 22, 1938, just before the Austrian Anschluss, the Czech National Alliance in Chicago,
then the small remnant of the erstwhile most important
element of the first resistance, issued a proclamation
from the pen of brother professor Jaroslav G. Mičan, in
order to concentrate forces toward the aid of threatened
Czechoslovakia. The occupation of Austria, after which
it was clear as daylight that German expansion would not
stop at the Austrian border, and the May mobilization of
the Czechoslovak armed forces, roused all larger settlements to public protests against nazism. They were held
in Chicago, Cleveland, New York, St. Louis, Detroit, Boston, Pittsburgh, Cedar Rapids, Omaha, St. Paul and in the
Texan towns. The speakers were leaders of our organizations, consuls and other representatives of Czechoslovakia
headed by ambassador Vladimír Hurban, and many American
officials. When the Czechoslovak government issued a call
for a defense fund of the republic, the kinsmen in America joined the drive with enthusiasm; collections were taken up automatically without central leadership everywhere, where our people lived. Contributions were sent
directly to Prague. This action was very much inspired
by the favorable attitude of the American press, which
with a few exceptions from the isolationist camp stood
on the side of threatened Czechoslovakia and sharply condemned the Nazi aggression in editorials and the news,
and also in splendid cartoons.

AMERICAN AID TO LIBERATE CZECHOSLOVAKIA

During World War II, the ethnic community
in America again aided the liberation movement of the ancestral homeland. The receipt
for one of the first checks, below, reads:
"President of Czechoslovak Republic. Receipt
for $ 25,000, i.e. twenty-five thousand
North-American dollars, which the Czech
National Alliance and the Czechoslovak
National Council in Chicago on February
15, 1941, handed to Dr. Jan Papánek as a
gift for the liberation action. London,
April 19, 1941. Signed: Dr. Edvard Beneš."

Source: Czech National Council Papers,
Czech and Slovak Immigration Archives,
University of Chicago.

PRESIDENT
ČESKOSLOVENSKÉ REPUBLIKY

P o t v r z e n í
----

na $ 25.000.-, t.j. dvacetpěttisíc severoamerických

dolarů, jež České Národní Sdružení a Československá

Národní Rada v Chicagu odevzdaly dne 15.února 1941

do rukou Dra Jana Papánka jako dar na osvobozovací

akci.

V Londýně, dne 19. dubna 1941.

Dr. Edvard BENEŠ.

RELEASE NO. 286
APRIL 23, 1945

News Flashes from Czechoslovakia

Published by the Czechoslovak National Council of America
4049 West 26th Street, Chicago 23, Ill., U. S. A.

Cooperating With the Czechoslovak Government Information Service

AMERICAN ARMY OF LIBERATION IN CZECHOSLOVAKIA

While the Russian armies are liberating Czechoslovakia from the east and driving from captured Bratislava have invaded Moravia, the American Army of liberation entered Czechoslovakia from the west.

The United Press reports from Paris, on April 18, that the American 3rd Army, completing its drive across the waist of Germany, invaded Czechoslovakia and advanced three miles into Bohemia, the western province of that country.

Lt. Gen. George Patton's tanks and infantry drove over the frontier at several points near Aš, in one of the four parts of Czechoslovakia awarded to Adolf Hitler under the Sudeten agreement drawn up at the 1938 Munich conference.

According to an Associated Press dispatch issued, on April 18, the first troops across the border were from the 3rd battalion of the 358th infantry of the 90th division, a battalion which had won a Presidential citation in the Mont Castre forest back in Normandy.

Two Americans of Czech ancestry were among the first American troops crossing into Czechoslovakia.

"My family came from this country," said Sgt. Joseph Joričák of Kansas City, Mo. "Look at those beautiful hills. I wish my folks could see them right now."

"My people have been in the United States twenty-four years, but I know they'd like to be here now and see the old homeland," mused Pvt. Elmer W. Hippik of Torrance, Calif.

Joričák and Hippik speak Czech, but they had no opportunity yet to use that language. The Sudeten German peasants living in that district are known for their fanatical adherence to the Nazi leader Konrad Henlein. They stolidly watched the 3rd Army push and seemed more frightened than friendly, says John R. Wilhelm, of the Chicago Sun Foreign Service.

MASARYK ON UNTIMELY DEATH OF PRES. ROOSEVELT

Jan Masaryk, Czechoslovak Minister of Foreign Affairs sent the following cables from London, on April 13:

To Mrs. Franklin D. Roosevelt: "You and yours have my deepest sympathy."

To Edward R. Stettinius, Jr.: "Am deeply grieved and shocked at the great and irreparable loss to all decent people on earth. Please convey to your colleagues, my Government's and my own deep sympathy."

Minister Masaryk also sent the following letters:

To Rudolf E. Schoenfeld, American Chargé d'Affaires to Czechoslovak Government: "May I, on behalf of my Government and myself, express the deepest possible sympathy to the American people who have lost a great first citizen. He was daring at a time when necessary. He knew long before Pearl Harbor America's place and gave everything and even more to this all-important purpose. He will be missed for a long time to come. The responsibilities of those who still are in the arena increased since yesterday. Let us hope that they and we will be found worthy when the real history of this shocking epoch is over."

To John S. Winant: "It is very difficult for me to imagine the present situation without Franklin Delano Roosevelt. I know how you felt about him, perhaps you know how I did. This is supposedly an official letter but I cannot be official today. His courage, his imagination, his conception of democracy, his voice and personality seemed absolutely essential yesterday. Today we must do without him. I hope we can. I am off to America tomorrow, as far as I am concerned, Washington will be different."

HURDLES OF COMMUNICATION

Věra Oravcová was a student when after
living through bombardments, underground
activities and concentration camps she
arrived in 1946 from Prague on a fellow-
ship to the University of Chicago to study American history. Her English was
shaky, and she was unacquainted with
the phraseology of the academic world
in the United States.

Source: One of Us, an American Journal,
unpublished, private collection.

    My cabin on the Liberty ship was so crowded, so
smelly with the sickness of about a dozen people, that
I slept for all ten days on a narrow wooden bench in the
writing room. Did that ship swing in the December waves!
There was no way to take a shower, I arrived in cold New
York all dirty, my coat wrinkled from sleeping in it. I
was glad nobody knew me. Yet--some woman at the pier
called my name, of which I understood only Veera, the
rest was scrambled in "Americanese" pronunciation. But
she found me all right; she worked for the Masaryk Institute and was my official greeter. As I was, she
dragged me to show me the stores of New York--how frus-
trating, I had hardly a dollar for food. I wanted to go
up the Empire State Building, because it was there--she
thought I was crazy, she was born in New York and never
was there. I had to get away. I pretended I was sick
and tired, so she put me on a bus to International House.
I got out the next stop and found my way to the Statue of
Liberty--THAT was the proper arrival in America!
    I spent Christmas at the home of old Czech settlers;
he was a retired steel-worker in a small town outside New
York. When we drove up to their house, I said it remin-
ded me of a "sport-house," not knowing the meaning of the
word; I meant chalet, a place you sleep in when you go
skiing or on a hike in the mountains. It was a house
built all of wood, so what else could it be? I thought
it was their summer and winter chalet for the holidays.
Inside, I got the surprise of my life: wall-to-wall car-
peting, piano--a steel-worker? There would be many
things in this America that I would have to learn.
    There was a whole convention of people, everybody
wanted to see the girl who was from the old country, who
met their son at the gate of her concentration camp.
Everybody was blabbering at once in a mixture of English
and Czech; some young men asked me repeatedly something
about a closet. Now, I knew that Americans were very

outspoken; but was it necessary for men to ask a young
lady if she had to go to the bathroom [closet in Czech
and several other languages means water closet]? I categorically said "no,"--and kept sitting in my coat. Finally the lady of the house took me upstairs and pointed
to two doors, mentioning again "closet." Do these people
have kidney troubles? They were obsessed with the bathroom. I was left alone; I opened one door, aha, there
it was, a small cubicle, some hangers on the walls, a
light switch; by now I was inspired to take the suggestion about the "closet," but where do you sit? This was
America; you probably push a button and it emerges from
the floor or the wall. No buttons. I hung my coat--and
thus started discovering America.

I arrived at the University of Chicago at registra-
tion time. As I had unlimited privileges at Charles University, I intended to take as many courses as possible
here. The adviser soon despaired over me; we had to con-
verse in French, for obvious reasons. I insisted on a
400 level course entitled "Problems in American History,"
a seminar for Ph.D. candidates; I was one, it even said
so on my calling card: "Cand. Phil.," which did not mean
a darned thing to him. He did not think I was ready for
it. After haggling for a while, I brought out my trump
card: "Aha, Monsieur, you just do not want foreigners to
find out what the problems are, n'est-ce pas?"

CZECH ATTITUDES TOWARD AMERICA

The Czechoslovak Society of America,
Č. S. A. for short, is the conglomer-
ation of several hundred benevolent
lodges all over the United States.
The first unit was founded in 1854.
Their attitude toward America is
spelled out in the following excerpt.

Source: Joseph Martínek, <u>Století</u> Jed-
<u>noty</u> Č. S. A., Cicero, Illinois, 1955.

For the fourth time in history, brothers of the Č.
S. A. fought for the American land of liberty and gave
not only of their labor and sweat but of their blood in
return for all that it gave them. This case in the history of the Č. S. A., the oldest of all Czecholsovak organizations, explains what is so striking and what obser-
vers and especially visitors from the old country find
hard to understand: why is it that Czechs in America do
not feel that they are in a foreign country, and especially, <u>why they do not consider themselves a national
minority in the European sense</u>, but an <u>indivisible and
natural component of the American nation</u>! The explana-
tion is simple: the Czechs started settling in smaller
groups and individually in this country since the earliest times; they had established a good name for themselves already during the colonial era. Their organized
and uninterrupted national activities in the United
States, as the existence of the Č. S. A. proves, have
been going on for a whole century.
For a hundred years they helped build this nation;
they gave it their hands and their sweat. They participated in the building of its great cities of millions,
in which they had settled as groups, when these cities
were but small and insignificant settlements. "They
broke the prairies" alongside native Americans and members of other nationalities; the history of the Middle
West is incomplete without the history of the Czech farmer on this last American frontier. They and their children fought for their country in all wars that the last
century had brought upon America. By the right of labor,
sweat and blood therefore, America is their homeland.
It belongs to them as much as to others who had helped
build America and fought for it; it is because of this
that they do not feel like strangers on American soil.

"DON'T PAVE THIS ROAD"

Joseph Martínek was born in Poděbrady
in 1889, at twenty immigrated to America. Metal worker by trade, he became a prominent labor leader and editor of Czech publications. Among other
works, he is the author of several collections of poetry in Czech and in
English. He lives in Tucson, Arizona.

Source: Joseph Martínek, <u>Songs</u> <u>of</u> <u>the</u>
<u>Desert</u>. New York, Universum Press, 1961.

Don't pave this road,
Don't cover its dust
With your fire-frozen dirt.

I like it as it is.
I like in this dust
To follow the soft tracks
Of barefooted Mexican kids,
Tracks of six little feet
Carrying three tough
Half-grown hearts
Filled
With one big idle afternoon
And a bit of eternity.

Don't pave this road
As you have covered up
So many soft tracks
Of little hearts
By the hard crust
Of your fire-frozen
Asphalt tainted civilization.

CZECHOSLOVAK SOCIETY OF ARTS AND SCIENCES IN AMERICA, INC.

381 PARK AVENUE SOUTH, ROOM 914, NEW YORK, N. Y. 10016

BULLETIN

VOL. 1, No. 1   MAY 1966

The Czechoslovak Society of Arts and Sciences in America

Its History and Activities

Before the Second World War it was comparatively rare for professional personnel to leave Czechoslovakia in order to settle permanently abroad. The German occupation, however, precipitated the departure or escape of about 20,000 persons, almost a quarter of them intellectuals. At war's end, some of this number naturally returned to their homeland, while others elected to remain abroad. Soon the ranks of the latter were swelled by a second exodus of more than 60,000 Czechoslovaks, following the Communist seizure of power in Prague during February 1948.

Precise statistics are, of course, hard to come by, but it is likely that there were, at mid-century, at least 6,000 writers, artists, musicians, intellectuals, and other professional Czechoslovaks living outside their country. Most of them settled in the United States, Canada, and Australia; others established themselves in Great Britain and Western Europe; smaller numbers found their way to Latin America, Asia, and Africa.

In 1958, a group of scholars led by Dr. Vaclav Hlavaty, Professor of Mathematics at the University of Indiana, and Dr. Jaroslav Nemec, of the National Library of Medicine, undertook to organize these Czechoslovak intellectuals throughout the world, in order to establish permanent and meaningful contact between them. At first this was an informal

(Continued on page 2)

AN INTRODUCTION AND EXPLANATION

In launching publication of this BULLETIN the Czechoslovak Society of Arts and Sciences hopes to offer an information service on the Society's programs and the activities of its many distinguished members. It will be the editorial policy of the BULLETIN to feature items of interest to members of the professions, the academic community, foundations, and institutions, both public and private. Accordingly, no attempt will be made to reproduce the detailed chronicle of the Society's work contained in its Czechoslovak-language monthly, ZPRAVY SVU. To be issued twice annually, in spring and fall, the BULLETIN is intended primarily for the Society's friends who cannot participate in its day-to-day activities.

Membership in the Society now exceeds 900, including scientists, teachers, lawyers, men of letters, artists, musicians, and members of the business community. Active branches of the Society may be found on virtually every continent, from the United States and Canada to Asia and Australasia, from Latin America to Great Britain and Western Europe. Many members have substantial achievements to their credit which deserve to be better reported and known.

The Society's past and present Presidents are both internationally recognized authorities: Professor Vaclav Hlavaty of the University of Indiana in the field of mathematics, and Professor René Wellek of Yale University in literary history and criticism. Both have given the Society consistently dynamic leadership,

which has been reflected in the vitality and constantly expanding range of its activities.

The Society is a cultural, non-political, and non-profit organization. It is dedicated to the encouragement of the broad and unfettered development of Czechoslovak culture in an atmosphere of freedom. Membership is open to individuals of Czechoslovak origin, to friends of Czechoslovakia, and to other oragnizations and associations sympathetic to the Society's aims.

The Society lends encouragement and support to the preparation of scholarly publications, sponsors lectures and other information programs, and maintains a documentation and reference service at its New York headquarters. It has also organized two cultural congresses, which are described elsewhere in this BULLETIN.

Since the BULLETIN seeks to bring these and other activities to the notice of a broader public, reactions and comments from recipients will be most welcome. By the same token, all members of the Society are particularly urged to communicate significant items of news to the Editor, including major publications, grants, academic honors, research projects, artistic or musical commissions, etc. Only through such cooperation can the BULLETIN become a useful channel of communication between the Society and its English-speaking friends, foundations, libraries, universities and colleges, and a broad range of other institutions.

R.B.

THE CZECHOSLOVAK NATIONAL COUNCIL
OF AMERICA
WHAT IT STANDS FOR

1918   1968

The Czechoslovak National Council of America is a non-profit patriotic organization of Americans of Czechoslovak descent. It came into being during World War I to coordinate the war effort of Americans of Czechoslovak origin who were determined, above all, to fulfill their duties as good Americans. Our forefathers also hoped to win independence for the country of their birth so that it too could enoy the same form of government and the same right to the pursuit of happiness with which they were blessed in their beloved United States.

Their war work was crowned with success and in the next twenty years they could point with pride to Czechoslovakia's great progress as a true democracy. During these two decades (1918-1938) the Council fostered a cultural program, promoted the teaching of Czech in American public schools and colleges, and sponsored other cultural activities.

This happy, peaceful period ended tragically at Munich by the sell-out of Czechoslovakia to Hitler. For the Czechoslovak National Council this was a signal for action on a grand scale. It immediately resumed its unifying role and again coordinated the war effort of Americans of Czechoslovak origin. It published "News Flashes" and brochures, organized mass meetings and headed various war drives, always working closely with the U.S. Government.

Unfortunately, Czechoslovakia was only half-free when the war ended and in 1948 the Communists, with Soviet assistance, seized complete power. The Council immediately grasped the significance of the Communist take-over not only for Czechoslovakia but for the entire free world. Since then the Council has tirelessly pointed out the tragic case of Czechoslovakia as a warning to alert American citizens to the Communist world threat. It publishes the Věstník, a monthly in Czech and Slovak, and a monthly newsletter the American Bulletin. Among its other publications are documentary brochures, the Czechoslovak Question in the United Nations by Dr. Jan Papánek, T. G. Masaryk and the Idea of World Federation by Dr. Peter Zenkl, Czechoslovakia in the Heart of Europe, and a very popular grammar Progressive Czech (fifth edition) by Prof. B. Mikula, etc.

The Council's main concern is to safeguard freedom. As its first duty it has successfully set out to unmask Communist attempts at infiltration of American organizations. Furthermore, it has warned Americans against Communist extortion rackets, such as Communist seizure of American legacies willed to Czechoslovak heirs. It has supported efforts to obtain a fair indemnity in U.S. dollars to American citizens for property seized in Czechoslovakia. Thus the Council has energetically tried to protect the interests and rights of American citizens.

Nationally, the Council has insisted on strict reciprocity in all U.S. agreements with the Prague government. For every American economic concession to the Communist regime it should give some political concession to its people to alleviate their suffering and injustices. The Council never forgets that the Czechoslovak people are our silent friends and their unrepresentative government our sworn enemy.

For 50 years the Council has helped to keep alive our Czechoslovak cultural heritage and our traditional love of freedom.

AN ASSERTION OF THE NEED TO INTENSIFY THE PURSUIT OF FREE INQUIRY AND EXCHANGE OF IDEAS*

PREAMBLE

The Czechoslovak Society of Arts and Sciences in America, Inc. (the Society), a nonpartisan, nonprofit, cultural organization, is dedicated to the principles of free search for truth and knowledge, free contacts among peoples and free dissemination of ideas. The Society associates scientists, scholars, artists, and writers throughout the world who, either because of their national origin or because of their particular interests and callings, pursue activities related to Czechoslovakia, her peoples and their contribution to the world culture.

RESOLUTION

Assembled in Washington, D.C. in commemoration of the Bicentennial Anniversary of the American Revolution, the members of the Society
- --Greatly cherishing their status as free men;
- --Proudly affirming their allegiance to the fundamental rights invested in the Declaration of Independence and the United States Constitution;
- --Sincerely joining in the celebration of the American Revolution;
- --Gratefully remembering the role of the American people in establishing a free and democratic Czechoslovakia;
- --Deservingly pointing out the contribution of Czechs and Slovaks to American and world culture;
- --Unwaveringly pledging their travail and endeavors to the cause of freedom and human dignity,

HAVE RESOLVED

TO REAFFIRM their faith in the free search for truth and individual happiness as the fundamental basis of any political system preserving the dignity of man;

TO EXPRESS their deep concern over the loss of freedom of assembly, inquiry and expression in Czechoslovakia and other countries of the world;

TO WELCOME the efforts of Czech and Slovak artists and scientists, dedicated to the principles of intellectual and creative freedom, who in the present difficult conditions in Czechoslovakia strive to fulfill their mission so important for all nations;

TO URGE all scientists, scholars, artists and writers throughout the world to ask and work for reestablishing of these fundamental rights in Czechoslovakia as well as elsewhere in the world;

TO CALL on all men of good will to join them and work together for application of the principles enunciated in the United Nations Universal Declaration of Human Rights and upholding universal belief in the worth and dignity of each human being.

*Approved by General Assembly of the Czechoslovak Society of Arts and Sciences in America, Washington, D.C. -- August 12, 1976.

Appendix 1.

CZECH AND CZECHOSLOVAK IMMIGRATION 1882 - 1975*

Year		Year		Year		Year	
1882		1901	3,766	1926	2,953	1951	3,863
1883	6,602	1902	5,590	1927	6,996	1952	5,041
1884	5,462	1903	9,577	1928	7,150	1953	2,173
1885	8,239	1904	11,838	1929	7,726	1954	2,235
1886	6,352	1905	11,757	1930	7,341	1955	1,983
1887	4,314	1906	12,953	1931	2,203	1956	2,612
1888	4,579	1907	13,554	1932	614	1957	3,541
1889	4,127	1908	10,164	1933	384	1958	2,156
1890	3,085	1909	6,850	1934	788	1959	2,813
1891	4,505	1910	8,462	1935	1,004	1960	2,391
1892	11,758	1911	9,223	1936	1,172	1961	1,978
1893	8,535	1912	8,439	1937	2,054	1962	1,691
1894	5,548	1913	11,091	1938	3,480	1963	1,845
1895	2,536	1914	9,928	1939	3,127	1964	1,666
1896	1,607	1915	1,651	1940	2,247	1965	1,894
1897	2,709	1916	642	1941	1,848	1966	1,463
1898	1,954	1917	327	1942	598	1967	1,406
1899	2,478	1918	74	1943	375	1968	1,678
1900	2,526	1919	105	1944	341	1969	3,307
	3,060	1920	415	1945	289	1970	4,520
		1921	1,743	1946	1,075	1971	1,799
		1922	12,542	1947	3,601	1972	1,783
		1923	13,840	1948	3,865	1973	1,552
		1924	13,554	1949	4,393	1974	683
		1925	2,462	1950	5,528	1975	525

* 1882-1921: Thomas Čapek, Čechs in America (Boston, 1920) and Tomáš Čapek, Naše Amerika (Prague, 1926). 1922-1956: Annual Report of the Commissioner General of Immigration; 1957-1975: Annual Report, Immigration and Naturalization Service; fiscal years ending June 30. Figures to 1921 are for Czechs only, from 1922 on for all Czechoslovakia.

Appendix 2.

CZECH IMMIGRANTS 1870, 1880, 1890, 1900 BY STATES
Source: Tomáš Čapek: Naše Amerika, Praha, 1926

STATE	1870	1880	1890	1900
Alabama	29	39	25	31
Alaska				8
Arizona Territory	2	7	3	16
Arkansas	21	68	97	281
California	90	239	243	504
Colorado	15	91	212	330
Connecticut	95	124	177	493
Delaware	1	2	3	4
District of Columbia	9	16	10	12
Florida	3	3	5	20
Georgia	33	33	35	23
Idaho	1	5	11	81
Illinois	7,350	13,408	26,627	38,570
Indiana	141	306	288	526
Indian Territory				24
Iowa	6,765	10,554	10,928	10,809
Kansas	105	2,468	3,022	3,039
Kentucky	40	43	58	52
Louisiana	23	24	14	30
Maine	1	1	3	16
Maryland	789	1,169	1,554	2,813
Massachusetts	110	279	581	810
Michigan	1,179	1,789	2,311	2,160
Minnesota	2,166	7,759	9,655	11,147
Mississippi	9	12	6	13
Missouri	3,517	3,342	3,255	3,453
Montana	23	25	198	177
Nebraska	1,770	8,858	16,803	16,138
Nevada	7	15	11	5
New Hampshire	4	10	3	11
New Jersey	271	429	306	1,063
New Mexico Territory	2	13	8	15
New York	2,071	8,748	9,129	16,347
North Carolina	5	14	11	3
North Dakota			1,129	1,445
Ohio	1,429	6,232	11,009	15,131
Oklahoma Territory			250	1,168
Oregon	36	109	79	231
Pennsylvania	580	1,058	2,031	3,368
Rhode Island	19	29	14	41
South Carolina	1	31	11	14
South Dakota	153	1,337	2,488	2,320
Tennessee	37	30	13	16
Texas	780	2,669	3,215	9,204
Utah	3	3	8	13
Vermont		4	10	27
Virginia	31	21	73	271
Washington	2	53	239	396
West Virginia	1	34	6	27
Wisconsin	10,570	13,848	11,999	14,145
Wyoming	8	10	31	58
Total:	40,287	85,361	118,197	156,809

Appendix 3.

DISTRIBUTION OF FIRST AND SECOND GENERATION CZECHS BY STATE

Source: Thirteenth Census of the U. S., 1910, and compilation from Thomas Capek, The Czechs in America, Boston, 1920. Figures in the first column indicate number of settlements with over 100 Czechs; all are enumerated by Capek.

STATE	CENTERS WITH OVER 100 CZECHS	1st & 2nd GENERATIONS	STATE	CENTERS WITH OVER 100 CZECHS	1st & 2nd GENERATIONS
Illinois	21	124,225	Montana	4	1,653
Nebraska	91	50,680	Virginia	5	1,059
Ohio	17	50,004	Arkansas	3	778
New York	19	47,400	Wyoming		671
Wisconsin	145	45,336	Idaho		663
Texas	154	41,080	West Virginia	1	535
Minnesota	55	33,247	Rhode Island		346
Iowa	47	32,050	Kentucky		305
Pennsylvania	18	13,945	Utah		268
Missouri	10	13,928	Alabama	1	184
Kansas	31	11,603	Tennessee		176
Michigan	7	10,130	New Mexico Terr.		175
South Dakota	41	9,943	Louisiana	3	173
Maryland	2	7,199	Washington, D.C.	1	135
North Dakota	13	7,287	Georgia		127
New Jersey	14	6,656	Delaware		121
Oklahoma	9	5,633	Arizona Terr.		97
California	3	3,707	Florida		92
Massachusetts	6	3,010	Nevada		84
Washington	3	2,984	South Carolina		71
Colorado	1	2,903	Mississippi		61
Connecticut	6	2,693	New Hampshire		44
Indiana	8	2,126	Maine		41
Oregon	4	1,709	North Carolina		16

Appendix 4.

GEOGRAPHIC DISTRIBUTION OF CZECHS IN THE UNITED STATES, 1910.*

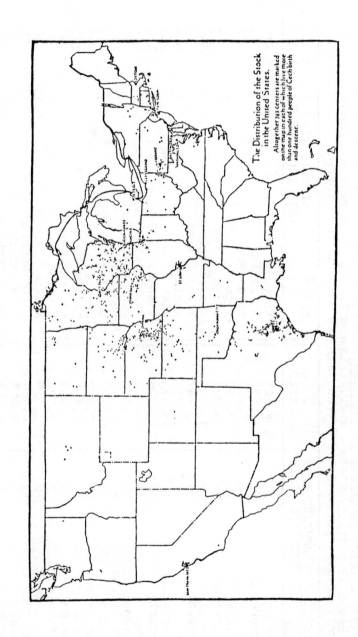

The Distribution of the Stock in the United States.

Altogether 742 centers are marked on the map in each of which live more than one hundred people of Czech birth and descent.

* Source: Thomas Čapek, Cechs in America, Boston, 1920.

Appendix 5.

SEX AND LITERACY OF SLAVIC IMMIGRANT ALIENS ADMITTED

FISCAL YEAR ENDED JUNE 30, 1911.

Source: Annual Report of the Commissioner General of Immigration to the Secretary of Labor, for the fiscal year ended June 30, 1911.

Nationality	Total admitted	Men	Women	Reads but not writes		Does not read or write	
				Men	Women	Men	Women
Czechs	9,223	5,214	4,009	3	3	89	35
Bulgarians, Serbians and Montenegrins	10,222	9,485	737	13		2,761	210
Croatians and Slovenians	18,982	13,466	5,516	19	2	3,347	1,132
Dalmatians, Bosnians and Hercegovinians	4,400	3,809	591			1,599	198
Poles	71,446	42,339	29,107	585	775	12,479	9,101
Russians	18,721	16,280	2,441	58	6	5,894	1,044
Ruthenians	17,724	11,375	6,349	33	24	5,070	2,862
Slovaks	21,415	13,173	8,242	18	14	2,613	1,472

Appendix 6.

CZECH CATHOLIC SCHOOLS IN THE UNITED STATES

Compared with the Slovaks or the
Poles, Czech Catholic schools lagged
behind. Part of the reason was the
strong voice of the freethinking
press. In 1924, when Czech ethnici-
ty in general started on the decline,
the numbers of teachers and pupils
were 385 and 16,447 respectively in
about seven dozen schools. Most teachers were nuns.

Source: Hlas (Voice), a calendar for
Czech Catholics in America, 1924.

State	teachers	pupils
Illinois (mostly Chicago)	67	3,341
Ohio (mostly Cleveland)	65	3,048
Texas	77	2,755
Minnesota	35	1,483
Nebraska	38	1,386
Wisconsin	16	924
Iowa	20	721
Maryland (mostly Baltimore)	11	665
Missouri (mostly St. Louis)	12	623
New York (mostly New York City)	19	529
Oklahoma	4	399
Pennsylvania	4	210
South Dakota	10	142
North Dakota	3	120
Michigan (mostly Detroit)	2	61
Virginia	2	40

Appendix 7.

RELIGIOUS PREFERENCES OF CZECHS

Under Austrian rule, 96% of Czechs were
counted as Catholics as the Protestant
faith had been proscribed. The Hussite
tradition was strong enough among the
history-conscious Czechs to prevent a
thorough Catholization. Once they arrived in America, the Czechs fell away
from the church, by conservative esti-
mates by 50-60%. In Chicago, their largest center, half of the Czechs were
non-churchgoers.

Source: Thomas Čapek, The Čechs in A-
merica, Boston, 1920.

---

1. New York City, 1920, per 1000 Czechs:

      254 Roman Catholics
      110 Protestants
       16 Jews
      620 without affiliation

---

2. United States, 1917:

a. Catholics: 320 centers*	b. Protestants: 160 centers**
68 Texas	43 Texas
57 Wisconsin	23 Pennsylvania
48 Nebraska	14 Nebraska
28 Minnesota	12 Illinois
21 Iowa	11 Ohio
16 Kansas	10 Iowa
14 Illinois	10 Minnesota
9 North Dakota	5 Kansas
7 Michigan	5 New York
6 Missouri	5 Wisconsin
6 Ohio	4 South Dakota
6 New York	3 Oklahoma
5 Oklahoma	2 Maryland
4 Maryland	2 Missouri
25 other	2 Virginia
	9 Other

* Some of these were Czecho-Irish or Czecho-Polish, etc.

** Pennsylvania centers were mostly Slovak. The break-
down of the denominations is: Presbyterian 55, Unity
of Czech and Moravian Brethren 30, Baptists 28, Methodists 21, Congregational 19, Independent Reformed 5,
Reformed Congregational 2.

Appendix 8.
CZECHOSLOVAKIA AFTER 1945*

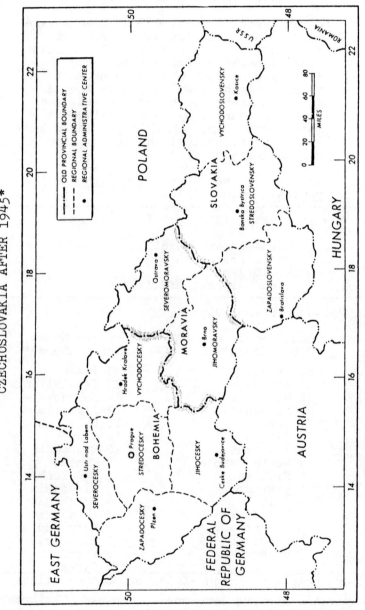

* Source: Eugene K. Keefe, et al. Area Handbook for Czechoslovakia. Washington, D.C., Government Printing Office, 1972. Population: 14 million; size: 49.4 square miles, about the size of North Carolina.

BIBLIOGRAPHY

The following bibliography is by necessity only a
fraction of what is available in libraries, local and
state historical societies and archives, not mentioning
private collections. The Czechs are a "bookish" people
and assiduous readers. An American historian describing
the settling of Texas wrote: "No immigrants brought
more books to the New World than did the Czechs." Even
taking this categorical statement with some reserve,
history bears out the fact that considering their relatively small number, the Czechs opened a floodgate of
publications, newspapers, almanacks, pamphlets and books.
During the first fifty years of their press in America,
they launched 340 periodicals, of which 90 were being
published in 1910. The several yearly almanacks are a
treasure-trove of historical reminiscences by early settlers, illuminating the Czech beginnings in America, and
at the same time throwing a light on the developmental
stages of the United States.

Reference books.

Jeřábek, Esther. Czechs and Slovaks in North America--
     A Bibliography. Washington, D. C. -Chicago, Czecho-
     slovak Society of Arts and Sciences in America -
     Czechoslovak National Council of America, 1976. (In-
     dispensable, 7600 entries with 1974 cut-off; still
     at press as of June, 1977.)

Meadowns, Paul et al. Recent Immigration to the United
     States. The Literature of the Social Sciences.
     Washington, D. C., Smithsonian Institution Press,
     1976.

U. S. Department of Commerce. Bureau of Census. His-
     torical Statistics of the United States. 2 vols.
     Washington, D. C., Government Printing Office, 1975.

U. S. Department of Justice. Immigration and Naturali-
     zation Service. Annual Report. Washington, D. C.,
     Government Printing Office, 1892- .

Wynar, Lubomyr R. Encyclopedic Directory of Ethnic News-
     papers and Periodical in the United States. Little-
     ton, Colorado, Libraries Unlimited, 1972.

In English: Books

Balch, Emily G. Our Slavic Fellow Citizens. New York,
     Charities Publications Committee, 1910.

Beneš, Eduard. My War Memoirs. Boston, Houghton Mifflin, 1928.

Brown, Francis J. & Roucek, Joseph S. One America. New York, Prentice-Hall, 1952.

Čada, Joseph. Czech-American Catholics, 1850-1920. Lisle, Illinois, Benedictine Abbey Press, 1964.

Čapek, Karel. President Masaryk Tells His Story. London, Allen & Unwin, 1934.

Čapek, Thomas. American Czechs in Public Office. Omaha, 1940.

_____. The Ancestry of Frederick Philipse. New York, 1939.

_____. Augustine Herrman of Bohemia Manor. Prague, 1930.

_____. The Čech (Bohemian) Community of New York. New York, Czechoslovak Section of America's Making, Inc., 1921. Contains listing of Czechs in New York 1847-1857.

_____. The Czechs and Slovaks in American Banking. New York, Fleming H. Revell, 1920.

_____. The Čechs (Bohemians) in America. Boston, Houghton Mifflin, 1920. Arno Press reprint, 1969. Indispensable to 1920.

Cather, Willa. My Antonia. Boston, Houghton Mifflin, 1918.

Directory and Almanach of the Bohemian Population of Chicago, 1915.

Dixon, S. H. and Kemp, L. N. The Heroes of San Jacinto. Houston, 1932.

Dvornik, Francis. Czech Contributions to the Growth of the United States. Lisle, Illinois, Benedictine Abbey Press, 1962.

Falge, Louis, ed. History of Manitowoc County, Wisconsin. 2 vols. Chicago, 1912.

Fermi, Laura. Illustrious Immigrants, The Intellectual Migration from Europe 1930-1941. Chicago, The University of Chicago Press, 1971.

Ginsburg, R. A., ed. and translator. The Soul of a Century. Collection of Czech poetry in English. 157 pp. Chicago, c. 1940.

Gottfried, Alex. Boss Cermak of Chicago. Seattle, University of Washington Press, 1962.

Handbook of Texas. Austin, Texas State Historical Association, 1952.

Houst, Anton P. The Czech Catholic Settlements in America. St. Louis, 1890.

Hudson, Estelle and Maresh, H. R. Czech Pioneers of the Southwest. Dallas, Southwest Press, 1934.

Hunt, C. L. et al. Ethnic Dynamics, New York, Dorsey Press, 1974.

Jelínek, Jarka and Zmrhal, Jaroslav. Sokol Educational and Physical Culture Association. Chicago, American Sokol Union, 1944.

Jičinský, J. R. ed. Tracing the History of the American Sokols, 1865-1908. Chicago, 1908.

Keefe, Eugene K. et al. Area Handbook for Czechoslovakia. Washington, Government Printing Office, 1972.

Kutak, Robert I. The Story of a Bohemian-American Village. Louisville, Kentucky, 1933.

Ledbetter, Eleanor. The Czechs of Cleveland. Cleveland, 1909.

Mallery, Charles P. Ancient Families of Bohemia Manor; their Homes and their Graves. Historical Society of Delaware, Wilmington, 1888.

Masaryk, Thomas G. The Making of a State: Memories and Observations, 1914-1918. London, 1927.

Mikula, B. Progressive Czech. Chicago, 1965.

Miller, Kenneth D. The Czecho-Slovaks in America. New York, G. Doran, 1922. Suffers from misconceptions.

Pergler, Charles. America in the Struggle for Czechoslovak Independence. Philadelphia, Dorrance, 1926.

Rechcigl, Miloslav, ed. Czechoslovak Contributions to World Culture. New York, Czechoslovak Society for Arts and Sciences in America, 1964.

Rechcigl, Miloslav. Czechoslovakia Past and Present.
    New York, Czechoslovak Society for Arts and Sciences
    in America, 1970.

Rosicky, Rose, comp. A History of Czechs (Bohemians) in
    Nebraska. Omaha, Czech Historical Society of Neb-
    raska, 1929.

Šiller, William et al. Memorial of Czech Evangelical
    Churches in the United States. Chicago, 1900.

Steiner, E. A. On the Trail of the Immigrant. New York,
    1906.

Stocker, Harry E. A History of the Moravian Church in
    New York City. New York, [1901?].

Thomson, Harrison S. Czechoslovakia in European History.
    Princeton University Press, 1943.

Voska, Emanuel V. and Irwin, Will. Spy and Counterspy.
    New York, Doubleday, Doran, 1940.

Vraz, Vlasta, comp. Panorama. Chicago, Czechoslovak
    National Council of America, 1970. Contains list
    of periodicals as of 1968.

Zeman, Zbynek. The Masaryks. New York, Harper and Row,
    1976.

Žižka, Ernest. Czech Cultural Contributions. Lisle,
    Illinois, Benedictine Abbey Press [?], 1937.

                    Articles and Pamphlets.

Bicha, Karel D. "The Czechs in Wisconsin History." Wis-
    consin Magazine of History, Madison, Spring, 1970.

_____. "The Survival of the Village in Urban America:
    A Note on Czech Immigrants in Chicago to 1914." In-
    ternational Migration Review, Spring, 1971.

Cross, R. D. "How Historians Have Looked at Immigrants
    to the United States." International Migration Re-
    view, Spring, 1973.

Doubrava, Ferdinand F. "Experiences of a Bohemian Emi-
    grant Family." Wisconsin Magazine of History, Madi-
    son, June 1925.

Hrbek, Sarah. "Bohemian Citizens Have Done Much for Cedar Rapids." The Cedar Rapids Sunday Republican,
   June 10, 1906.

Hrbková, Šárka B. "Bohemians in Nebraska." Publications,
   Nebraska State Historical Society, Lincoln, 1919.

Hrdlička, Aleš. "Bohemia and the Czechs." National Geographic Magazine, February, 1917.

James, James A. "The Yankees of Central Europe." Century Magazine, October, 1922.

Jonáš, Charles. "The Bohemians of Chicago." Chicago
   Sunday Times, January 24, 1892.

Kohlbeck, V. "Bohemians in the United States." Cham-
   plain's Educator, January-March, 1906.

Mamatey, Victor S. "Building Czechoslovakia in America
   1914-1918." Czechoslovak Society of Arts and Sciences in America, 1976.

Masaryk, Alice G. "The Bohemians in Chicago." Charities, December 3, 1904.

Mashek, Nan. "Bohemian Farmers of Wisconsin." Charities, December 3, 1904.

Matthews, Albert. "Comenius and Harvard College." Publications, Colonial Society of Massachusetts, March,
   1919.

Rechcigl, Miloslav. "Ten Years of the Czechoslovak Society of Arts and Sciences in America, Inc." New
   York, The Society, 1966.

Robbins, Jane E. "The Bohemian Women in New York."
   Charities, December 3, 1904.

Roucek, J. S. "The Image of the Slav in United States
   History and in Immigration Policy." American Journal of Economics and Sociology, January, 1969.

_____. "The Passing of American Czechoslovaks."
   American Journal of Sociology, March, 1934.

_____. "Problems of Assimilation: A Study of Czecho-
   slovaks in the United States." Sociology and Social
   Research, September-October 1932.

Schonberg, Harold C. "Even the Prima Donna Blushed."
   New York Times, November 23, 1969.

Scott, F. D. "The Peopling of America: Perspectives on Immigration." American Historical Association, Pamphlet # 241, Washington, 1972.

Shwehla, J. "Bohemians in Central Kansas." Colections, Kansas State Historical Society, Topeka, 1913-1914.

Smith, T. L. "New Approaches to the History of Immigration in the 20th Century America." American Historical Review, July, 1966

Spinka, Matthew, ed. "John Amos Comenius, The Bequest of the Unity of Brethren." Chicago, National Union of Czechoslovak Protestants, 1940.

Taggart, Glen L. "Czechs of Wisconsin as a Culture Type." University of Wisconsin Ph.D. dissertation, 1948.

Vlach, J. J. "Our Bohemian Population." Proceedings, Wisconsin State Historical Society, Madison, 1902.

                    In Czech: Books

Beneš, Vojta. Masarykovo dílo v Americe (Masaryk's Work in America). Prague, 1923.

Bubeníček, Rudolf, comp. Dějiny Čechů v Chicagu (History of Czechs in Chicago). Chicago, by the author, 1939. Contains listing of all Czechs to 1871.

Čapek, Tomáš. Moje Amerika, vzpomínky a úvahy 1861-1934 (My America, Reminiscences and Reflections 1861-1934), Prague, Fr. Borový, 1935.

_____. Naše Amerika (Our America), Prague, Orbis, 1926.

_____. Padesát let Českého tisku v Americe (Fifty Years of Czech Press in America). New York, Board of Trustees of Bank of Europe, 1911.

_____. Památky Českých emigrantů v Americe (Monuments of Czech Immigrants in America). Omaha, Národní tiskárna, 1907. Contains listing of periodicals 1860 - 1910.

Čermák, J. Dějiny občanské války (History of the Civil War), Chicago, 1889.

Dvořák, Josef A. Dějiny Čechů ve státu South Dakota (History of Czechs in the state of South Dakota). Tabor, South Dakota, 1920.

Habenicht, Jan A. Dějiny Čechův amerických (History of American Czechs). St. Louis, 1910.

_____. Z pamětí Českého lékaře (Memories of a Czech doctor). Chicago, 1897.

Habrman, Gustav. Z mého života (From My Life). Prague, 1914.

Houšt, A. P. Krátké dějiny a seznam českých katolických osad (Brief History and List of Czech Catholic Settlements). St. Louis, 1890.

Klíma, Stan. Čechové a Slováci za hranicemi (Czechs and Slovaks Abroad). Prague, J. Otta, 1925.

Kozák, Jan B. T. G. Masaryk a Vznik Washingtonské Deklarace v říjnu 1918 (T. G. Masaryk and the Origin of the Washington Declaration in October 1918), Prague, Melantrich, 1968.

Martínek, Joseph. Století Jednoty Č.S.A. 1854 - 1954 (One Hundred Years of the Czechoslovak Society of America). Cicero, Illinois, The Society, 1955.

Odložilík, Otakar. Obrázky z dvou světů (Vignettes from Two Worlds). Philadelphia, Sklizeň svobodné tvorby, 1958.

Rosická, Růžena. Dějiny Čechů v Nebrasce (History of Czechs in Nebraska). Omaha, Český historický klub, 1928.

Vojan, J. E. S. Česko-americké epištoly (Czecho-American Epistles). Chicago, 1911.

Periodicals.

Duben, Vojtěch N. "České a slovenské noviny a časopisy v zahraničí v září 1970" ("Czech and Slovak newspapers and magazines abroad in September 1970). New York, Czechoslovak Society for Arts and Sciences in America, 1970. Mimeographed.

Americké listy (American Gazette), [New York] Perth Amboy, N. J., weekly, 1962- .

Amerikán-Národní kalendář (The American-National Calendar). Chicago, annual, 1878-1957.

Dělnické listy (Workmen's Gazette). Cleveland, New York, weekly, daily, 1875-1883, 1893-1898.

Denní Hlasatel (Daily Crier). Chicago, daily, 1891- .

Dennice novověku (Morning Star of New Era). Cleveland, weekly, bi-weekly, 1877-1917?

Hlas Jednoty (Voice of Union). Chicago, weekly, monthly, quarterly, 1947- .

Hlas Jednoty svobodomyslných (Voice of Freethinkers' Union). Iowa City, New York, Chicago, monthly, 1872-1881.

Hospodář (Husbandman). Omaha, monthly, 1891-1961.

Kalendář Národ (Calendar [of] Nation). Chicago, annual, 1949- ; successor of Katolík (The Catholic), 1895-1948.

Květy Americké (American Flowers). Omaha, monthly, weekly, 1884-1887, 1900-1903, 1916-1919.

Národ (Nation). Chicago, daily, weekly, 1894-1975.

New Yorské listy (New York Gazette). New York, daily, thrice weekly, 1874-1966 with interruption. Merged with Americké listy, 1966.

Pokrok Západu (Progress of the West). Omaha, weekly, bi-weekly, 1871-1915.

Proměny (Metamorphoses). New York, Washington, D. C., quarterly, 1964- .

Sion almanach (Zion Almanac [of Protestants]). Pittsburgh, annual, 1901-1917.

Slávie (Slavia). Racine, Chicago, weekly, 1861-1946.

Sokol Americký (American Sokol). Chicago, monthly, 1879- .

Svornost (Concord). Chicago, daily, 1875-1957.

Věk rozumu (Age of Reason). New York, Chicago, monthly, 1910- .

Ženské listy (Women's Gazette). Chicago, weekly, monthly, 1894-1947.

Zprávy S.V.U. (News of the Czechoslovak Society of Arts and Sciences in America). New York, Washington, D. C., monthly, 1959- .